T0130511

# RESPECT AND RECOGNITION
## OF THE FINEST FIGHTING UNIT
## OF THIS COUNTRY

Norman G. Albert

Order this book online at www.trafford.com
or email orders@trafford.com

Most Trafford titles are also available at major online book retailers.

Printed in the United States of America.

ISBN: 978-1-4669-2994-4 (sc)
ISBN: 978-1-4669-2993-7 (e)

Library of Congress Control Number: 2012906987

*Trafford rev. 04/27/2013*

 www.trafford.com

**North America & international**
toll-free: 1 888 232 4444 (USA & Canada)
phone: 250 383 6864 ♦ fax: 812 355 4082

VALOR

BRAVERY

COURAGE

BOLDNESS

GALLANTRY

DUTY

EMPER-FI

I dedicate this manuscript to the many Marines who were not respected or recognized as a member of the finest unit of the Armed Services

# PRELUDE

In the spring of 1944, three of my friends and I went to Boston to join the Marine Corps to fight for our country. Bob Lucas failed his physical and was accepted into the Seabees. He was attached to the 5th Marine Division and participated in the invasion of Iwo Jima. Alfred Quinty also failed his physical and was accepted in the Navy where he served on the USS Johnson in the North Atlantic. Bob Cormier passed his physical and was accepted and made a career of the Marine Corps and participated in World War II, Korea and Viet Nam. I failed my physical because I had developed a hernia. At the time, I was a welder on liberty ships in South Portland, Maine, and because of my experience as a welder they wanted to take me in the Seabees immediately and they would operate on me. My heart was always on being a Marine so I said "no" and that I would return home, have surgery, and then return to join the Marines Corps. I returned later in 1944 and passed my physical and was accepted. I reported to Parris Island for boot camp and then to Camp LeJeune for advance training. I could not wait to fulfill my duty to fight for my country.

My disappointment came when most of my platoon was transferred to Camp Pendleton and, as far as I know, took part in the invasion of Okinawa. I was in a group which was transferred to Quantico, Virginia, and then to Dahlgren, Virginia, for guard duty. When you are in the Marines, you must follow orders. While doing Stateside duty, the war ended and I was denied the honor of joining my buddies from our platoon to fight for my country. This has always been a big disappointment in my life, even to this day as I turn 85 years old. In December of 1945, I was transferred to Camp Pendleton, California, for more training and fire watch. In February of 1946, I was ordered to board the Liberty Ship, USS Starlight, to go to China and join the 1st Marine Division with the mission of disarming the Japanese soldiers and return them to Japan Proper.

During my duty in China, among other things like standing Guard duty, I was part of convoys delivering needed supplies to our forces in Peking (Beijing). The Chinese Communist soldiers would attack our convoys. Marines were wounded, killed and taken prisoner. Fortunately, none of the convoys that I drove were attacked.

In 2011, I wrote a book entitled <u>YOHOUSE, FROM A BOOT TO A CHINA MARINE</u> which recorded my experiences of my duty in China.

I have read many books about the war in the Pacific, from Guadalcanal to Okinawa and Korea, and while reading about the many struggles that the Marine Corps went through to maintain the Marine Corps as a fighting unit and decided to write this book.

It is amazing what Presidents and Navy Admirals did and what Army Generals continue to this day, to attempt to disrespect the finest fighting unit called the Marine Corps.

I would like to state at the beginning of this book that I have enormous respect for all Army soldiers, Navy sailors and U.S. Airmen who have served their country with dignity and honor. Some of my relatives and friends have distinguished themselves in their services. My uncle was killed in World War I at Chateau Thierry and my father-in-law was wounded in the same battle.

I have read many books about the battles that were fought by our service members throughout history, and I'm amazed at how some Presidents, Army Generals and Navy Admirals have attempted to reduce and, at times, tried to eliminate the Marine Corps altogether.

This story should be told to educate the public about the plight of the Marine Corps to maintain their existence as a unique and valuable service to fight for their country.

I will quote many times from the book <u>FIRST TO FIGHT</u> by Victor H. Krulak whose book should be required reading by all Marines and anyone who would understand what the Corps has undergone to survive as a fighting unit. Many Marine Generals and many generations of Marines before him who have learned through hard experiences that fighting for the right to fight often presented greater challenges than fighting the enemy. While quoting from these books, I will paraphrase some areas without changing the meaning of the text. I will not quote everything they have written but will glean in areas throughout their books. They have thoroughly explained, in detail, the problems that the Marine Corps and its officers went through to preserve this great institution.

Also quoting from the book <u>FOR COUNTRY AND CORPS</u>, the life of General Olive P. Smith by Gail Shisler, of General Smith's frustration while fighting in Korea with Army Generals such as General Douglas MacArthur and General Edward Almond's continual interferences with preforming his duty, and protecting his 1<sup>st</sup> Marine Division from being destroyed by the Chinese Army

I will also quote from the book <u>DEVIL DOGS AT BELLEAU WOOD</u> by Dick Camp, and also <u>AMERICAN CAESAR, DOUGLAS MACARTHUR</u> by William Manchester.

According to Victor Klulak in his book <u>FIRST TO FIGHT</u> the Army began its onslaught against the Marine Corps in 1942 after Guadalcanal in a meeting in Hawaii where General J.L. Collins stated that the Army was resolved to eliminate forever its deficiencies in amphibious matters and its dependencies on Marines for amphibious expertise. He stated that the Army would master these exercises, which were not difficult. Then in New Caladonia General Collins Condemned the operation of the Navy and Marines at Guadalcanal and stated that the Marines should not have been there and organized steps were under way to preclude the Marines from further preempting the function of the other services. This statement is amazing when you read about what the Navy did to the Marines when they landed on Guadalcanal to stop the advance of the Japanese in the Pacific. Quoting from the book <u>BRUTE</u> by Robert Coram, the Joint Chief of Staff and America's Pacific commanders wondered whether the Marines were up to the task.

General MacArthur, usually the most optimistic of battle commanders, said success at Guadalcanal "was open to the gravest doubts." Admiral Robert L. Ghormley, the overall on-scene Navy Commander, said the battle would be "attended with the gravest risk" and wanted the invasion postponed. But fate and destiny were colliding, and the fight was on. The Marines, led by Alexander A. Vandergrift, still carried the vintage Springfield .03 rifles. 2 months after the Marines landed on Quadacanal, the 164th Army Regement landed to reinforce the Marines who had been fighting an overwhelming force of Japanese soldiers. The Army arrived with the new semi-automatic Garand M-1 rifles. Many Marines would have been saved if they had been issued the M-1 rifles to fight the enemy. The Army was issued these M-1 rifles in the United States for training. There are few examples of major military operations begun and carried out under such unfavorable conditions as at Guadalcanal. The Navy launched the landing crafts six miles off shore, a by-the-book maneuver designed to keep the large ships beyond the reach of medium-range Japanese Artillery. But the Japanese had no medium-range artillery and each wave of landing craft took two hours to go from ship to shore.

The long ship-to-shore movement was only the beginning of Marine troubles. After the Marines landed and established a beachhead, it would take several days to unload their food and equipment—everything from artillery pieces to bulldozers.

But the morning of the landing, Admiral Frank J. Fletcher, whose aircraft carrier supported the invasion, announced that his ship did not have enough fuel. He sailed away, followed a day later by the supply ships, leaving the Marines with only half of its supplies of ammunition, food and equipment including artillery pieces and bulldozers. The navy under Admiral Fletcher, had abandoned the Marines on a hostile shore of Guadalcanal without protection and without all their supplies.

Samuel E. Morris, the great historian of World War II, said that Fletcher "could have remained in the area with no more consequences than a sunburn." The Navy had abandoned the Marines on a hostile shore. To Krulak, Guadalcanal was blood-etched proof of everything Smith had told him about the Navy's attitude toward the Marines, and more than sixty years later, Krulak still expressed resentment that the Navy had abandoned the Marines on the shores of Guadalcanal without sufficient supplies and equipment. This resentment remains almost universal in the Marine Corps even to this date.

In 1999, John Keenan, now a retired Colonel and editor of the Marine Corps Gazette and Director of the Expeditionary Warfare School, that trains officers, a Naval officer asked him when the Marines would forgive the Navy for Guadalcanal. "The twelfth of Never." He said.

Another occasion took place in Washington D.C. in 1943 where Army Chief of Staff George C. Marshall presented to the Joint Chief of Staff his concept of a unified Defense Department including a separate Air Force, where a single Chief of Staff and an armed forces general staff would manage all the nation's military affairs. It would consist of Army, Navy and Air Force. No mention was made of the Marine Corps. This would eliminate any civilian control.

In 1945, Marine General Merrill B. Twinning realized the Army's design on the Marines, had Victor Krulak transferred to Washington D.C. where they formed the Chowder Society that worked outside of the normal channels. They felt strongly that preservation of the unquestioned civil authority over military affairs be maintained to preserve the Marine Corps.

The Marine anti-unification organization made itself felt for the first time through a statement to the Senate Committee by Marine Commander Alexander A. Vandergrift. In 1945, he attacked the proposed invasion of the civilian sphere by the military, the erosion of congressional influence over military affairs and control of the budget by the supreme Military Commander. This was an open declaration that survival of the Marine Corps as an anti-institution was the center of the Army sights to eliminate the Marine Corps. Lieutenant General Roy S. Geiger spoke very bluntly to the committee and strongly opposed the legislation strongly.

When finished, the subcommittee and the press viewed General Geiger's testimony as the classic Marine style. He put the Army on notice that the Marines were not going to take lying down the humiliation planned for them. The trouble deepened in 1945 when President Truman sent a message to Congress stressing his desire to see a reorganization of the military along the lines recommended by the War Department. He declared that the Marine Corps should be a part of the Navy. He described the Marine Corps as a duplication of the Army and as the Navy's own little army that talks Navy and is known as the Marine Corps.

Generals George C. Marshall and Dwight Eisenhower said that the Marines were bent on creating a second land Army. General Eisenhower, the Army Chief of Staff, declared that the Marines had merely duplicated the role of the Army function in the recent war. He proposed to the (JCS) Joint Chief of Staff a new function for the Marine Corps: the Marines should only operate landing crafts, and that the Marines should not exceed the size of a regiment and not to be expanded in the time of war. An Army memorandum challenging the importance of close air support as nourished by the Marines, and denied that the Marines had carried the burden of the amphibious march across the Pacific and that the Army had indeed been ready to take part in the amphibious war in the Pacific from the start.

General Alexander Vandergrift delivered bill #2044, that would give the War department authorization to reduce the Marine Corps to a position of a military insignificance a shattering blow. He stated that this bill gives the War Department a free hand with its expressed desire to reduce the Marine Corps to a position of military insignificance. Secretary of Defense and the all-powerful National Chief of Staff are free to either abolish the Marine Corps outright or eliminate it from all its vital function. He followed up by noting that the United States possessed the world's top ranking Marine Corps at an annual cost of $1500 per Marine as opposed to the cost of $2500 per soldier. He believed it had earned this right to have its future decided by the Legislative body, which created it, nothing more. The bended knee is not a tradition of our Corps. If the Marine as a fighting man has not made a case for himself after 170 years, then he must go. But I think you will agree with me that he has earned the right to depart with dignity and honor, not by subjugation to the status of usefulness and servility planned for by the War Department. The implicit challenge to the authority of Congress surfaced and the proposed single Chief of Staff was widely condemned.

President Harry Truman was stunned by the adverse publicity and the congressional reaction to the measure that he abandoned it. To salvage something, he directed the Secretary of War Robert Peterson and Secretary of Navy James Forrestall to get together on the merger issue. They tried with the exclusion of the Marines and they failed. The Army was still adamant claiming that the Marine Corps was an unnecessary duplication of the Army's rightful combat role.

In January of 1947, a joint letter from Secretaries Robert Peterson, Secretary of War and James Forrestall, Secretary of the Navy to President Truman saying they reached a full accord on a form, which our National Security Organization should take, that of a single Military Commander. It retained the idea of three military departments, Army, Navy and Air Force and a Joint Chief of Staff supported by a full Joint staff and a Secretary of Defense with Authority over both the Military Departments and Joint Chiefs. There was nothing that told what the individual Military Services would do and nothing that insured the existence of the Marine Corps in anything more than a name.

In that connection, the joint letter declared that the roles and mission of the several Armed Forces should be prescribed by an Executive Order, leaving to the discretion of the President or the Secretary of Defense, what any service might be called to do. The law generally covered the Army, Navy and the Air Force as were the positions of Defense Secretary and a Joint Chief of Staff. But as General Edson stated, "a President so disposed could eliminate the effectiveness of the Marine Corps by the stroke of a pen." There was a need to educate Congress and the media to the realities of the problem.

The Marines had allies in the Marine Corps reserve officers, the American Legion and the Veterans of Foreign Wars to explain to Congress about the problem. They learned that the bill would be heard by the Army dominated Armed Service Committee.

In February, without a shred of Marine impute, they learned that General Eisenhower had no reluctance to voice his support for the German political-military system. The Under Secretary of War, Kenneth Royall, echoed General Eisenhower's statement. The bill was then passed in the Senate. The Veterans of Foreign Wars took a positive stand with regard to the continuance of the Marine Corps. The organization urged Congress to amend the proposed unification bill to the end that the future duties of the Marine Corps and the part that they shall play in the Armed Forces are spelled out and not left dangling in space subject to the possible whims of inter-service intrigue.

President Truman made known to Secretary of the Navy James Forrestall and Secretary of War, Robert Peterson his dissatisfaction with the lobbying of the military Services, telling General Vandergrift to keep the Naval and Marine Corps off the hill and keep them off.

President Truman's obvious dissatisfaction with anti-merger lobbying produced a reverse of his desired effect. Members of the Committee complained of what they described as a "gag" placed almost exclusively on military opposition to the legislation, saying that they were being permitted to hear only one side of the argument. Ultimately, and with Secretary Forrestall, suspended the provisions of Navy regulations that stood in the way of open opposition by Navy and Marine officers. They were strongly opposed to the measure.

The testimony of Brigadier Merritt A, Edson of the Marine Corps was a powerful witness. It distilled all the thoughts and arguments that the violence done by the pending bill to civilian control of the military establishment. He condemned any system that would place a third of our national budget in the hands of a defense secretary whose staff was predominantly military and whose charter permitted unlimited expansion, were soberly expressed by Congressman Clare E. Hoffman were as follows:

*   That there be no Secretary of Defense serving as an advocate to the head of the military establishment; rather that there be a presidential deputy to speak for the president in resolving problems affecting the military departments.

* That the military influence in the National Security Council and Central Intelligence Agency presently provided for in the bill be removed.
* That the size and function of the Joint Staff be rigidly delineated, and converted to a secretariat.
* That the roles and mission of all the Armed Forces be spelled out in law.

The house version passed and President Truman signed it into law. There was protection for Naval Aviation and the role and mission of the Marine Corps was as follows: The Marine Corps shall be organized, trained and equipped to provide fleet marine forces of combined arms together with supporting air components, for service with the fleet in the seizure or defense of advanced naval bases and for the conduct of such land operations as may be essential to the prosecution of a naval campaign. In a conversation with Commandant Alexander Vandergrift at the height of the controversy, the president eyed him quizzically and said, "You Marines don't trust anybody do you?" The President was right.

The Army was very unhappy with the legislation. It had fallen far short of attaining their objectives. The defining roles and missions, which included Marine Corps protection, was a visible affront and an irritation, but more disappointing to the Army was the failure to achieve the broader organizational goals. Instead of a highly centralized arrangement where a singular military leadership could confidently face budgetary problems with no fear of internal military dissention, the Army ended up with no Chief of Staff, a sharply circumscribed General Staff, and a Defense Secretary with loosely defined jurisdiction. The open charter of the Defense Secretary could, in fact, turn out to be the greatest problem of all in the years to follow, not for just the Army but for all the services. The Marine Corps always favored more rather than less civilian control so that the military might confine itself to the planning and direction of combat operations.

Thus the law, which so much sweat had been expended, was as best a fragile mutation. At no surprise to the Marine Corps, the centralization advocates initiated a move to advance a step nearer their goal. General Eisenhower fired the opening shot on the occasion of his retirement as Chief of Staff of the Army in 1948. In a long and sober memorandum to Secretary Forrestal, he voiced his concern with various aspects of the organization for national security, among them the circumscribed scope of the Joint Chief of Staff as he saw it and the invasive character of the Marine Corps, where the Army was concerned.

The size of the Secretary of Defense's office and the increases of his authority and control over the "departments and agencies of the National Military

Establishment" and also at the prompting of General Eisenhower, proposes the creation of a chairman of the Joint Chiefs of Staff and an increase of the size of its staff.

A subcommittee on efficiency in the Federal Government echoed these proposals, as did President Truman as a workable basis for beginning the unification of the military services and a proposal that the departments of the Army, Navy and Air Force be downgraded to military departments. Secretary Forrestal brought together high-ranking defense officials to hammer out details of the services' roles and missions. The Marine Commandant was not included. The conference spoke primarily about what the Marines would not do.

*   The Corps would not expand beyond four-divisions wing strength in time of war (despite its obvious capability to do more as exemplified by World War II.)
*   The Corps would not be permitted to exercise command above the Corps level (evidently to counter what the Army had regarded as a threat in World War II).
*   The Corps would not be permitted to create a second land army (it was not lost on the Marines that these same words had appeared in General Eisenhower's memorandum to the Joint Chiefs of Staff in 1946.

Parallel with these actions was a trend to diminish steadily the personnel strength and combatant capability of the Marine Corps. The defense secretary in his 1959 budget, decreed that the Marine Corps be cut from 100,000 to 6,500 men, Its infantry force be cut from 11 to 8 battalions, and its aviation squadrons from 33 to 12. Congress promoted legislation that would make the Commandant of the Marine Corps a member of the Joint Chiefs. General Gates outspokenly supported the congressional movement. He said that without the Joint Chiefs position the Marine Corps did not have adequate representation in matters of vital concern both to the Marine Corps itself and to the National Defense. General Gates told Congress "the power of the budget, the power of coordination and the power of strategic direction of the Armed Forces have been used as devices to destroy the operating forces of the Marine Corps."

The adverse effects of this policy of exclusion and administrative starvation were dramatically illuminated by the disadvantaged size and condition of the Marine operating forces at the onset of the Korean Conflict. The situation reinforced the ongoing pressure to see a law passed that would protect the personnel strength of the Marine Corps, and place its Commandant on the Joint Chief of Staff.

The victory of the Marines against the North Koreans in 1950 in the Pusan Perimeter in the Korean conflict inspired Congressman McDonough to write a letter to President Truman praising the Marines' battlefield performance over the years and applauding their valiant response to the Korean crisis. President Harry Truman rubbed raw by the widespread attacks on him and his administration. As exemplified by McDonough's letter, he vented his frustration on the Marines for whom he had little love anyhow. He wrote McDonough a furious response which, imprudently, he put the Marine Corps in its place-as he saw it "For your information" he wrote, "the Marine Corps is the Navy's police force and as long as I am President, that is what it will remain. They have a propaganda machine that is almost equal to Stalin's."

The Truman letter became public knowledge when McDonough inserted it in the Congressional record. And the fat was in the fire. Senators and Representatives on both sides of the aisle excoriated the President's comment. The press followed suit with articles and editorials. There was the heaviest mail and telegrams from private citizens to the White House protesting Truman's letter. At that time, the Marine Corps League was holding its convention in Washington. It resolved to demand that the President apologize to the American people for his insult to the Marine Corps. Because of the public outcry and counsel from his staff, he put his signature to a carefully qualified letter of apology to Commandant Gates. "I sincerely regret the unfortunate choice of language which I used in my letter to Congressman McDonough. I am certain that the Marine Corps itself does not indulge in such propaganda." He delivered this letter in person to Commandant Robert Gates along with his regrets. Truman's Press Secretary urged the President to appear before the Marine Corps League. After some confusion, Truman decided to address the Marine Corps League. The League, with its fierce loyalty to the Marine Corps, had cause for concern on how it would react if the President were to appear before them? The President spoke at length about the Korean War, his aspiration for peace and his respect for the Marine Corps. The League responded with unusual dignity and, on his departure, voted unanimously to accept the President's apology.

Senator Paul Douglas and congressman Mike Mansfield sponsored a bill providing that the Marine Corps be composed of four combat divisions and four aircraft wings and that the Commandant of the Marine Corps be a member of the Joint Chief of Staff. The Secretary of Defense and the Joint Chief of Staff opposed the bill. The bill was enacted and the legislation provided that the Marine Corps shall be organized so as to include not less than three combat divisions and three aircraft wings. The Commandant of the Marine Corps shall indicate to the Chairman of the Joint Chief, any matters scheduled for consideration that directly concern the Marine Corps, and that the

Commandant has co-equal status with the members of the Joint Chiefs of Staff.

In the preamble, the law declared that the United States Marine Corps was and has been a separate military service like all the others, serving within the Department of the Navy along with the Navy. Secretary of Defense Robert Lovett recommended this to the commission with Eisenhower's approval.

In 1953, the committee sent to Congress a reorganization plan plus a few items along the way. President Eisenhower proposed that selection of the Director of the Joint Staff should be subject to the approval of the Secretary of Defense and that the Joint Staff be managed by the Chairman and not by the corporate Joint Chiefs.

The reorganization plan No.6 debate was scarcely ended when it received a challenge from the Navy; it stated that the Secretary of the Navy wanted to clarify the responsibilities of the Commandant of the Marine Corps to the Secretary of the Navy. The Chief of Naval operation, Admiral Forrest R. Sherman, offered four propositions to apply in a redraft to General Order No. 5.

\* That the Marine Corps do not possess operating forces; all Marine Corps combat units being ipso facto a part of the operating forces of the U.S. Navy.

22

* That the chief of naval operations should exercise general and direct supervision over the Headquarters of the Marine Corps.
* That the chief of naval operations enjoys a broad authority over the entire Department of the Navy, including the Marine Corps. In other words, he commands the Marine Corps, its forces and its headquarters and has the authority to establish the Corps requirements for both men and material

Commandant Lemuel Shepherd took strong issue with this position. Secretary Thomas directed that the Chief of Naval Operations and the Commandant of the Marine Corps resolve the problem. Being unable to reach an agreement, each offered his own wording of the question of personnel and material requirement. After deliberations, Secretary Robert Anderson found in favor of the Marines, approving the key wording as follows. The Commandant of the Marine Corps is the senior officer of the United States Marine Corps. He commands the Marine Corps and is directly responsible to the Secretary of the Navy for its administration, discipline, internal organization, unit training, requirements, efficiency, and readiness, and for the total performance of the Marine Corps. It was a victory for the Marine Corps and it stood up for almost three decades.

President Eisenhower, disgruntled that his goal had not been met, set in motion two new studies.

Both addressed the same targets as earlier. Although Congress had rebuffed him before, he asked again that the restrictions be removed from the Defense Secretary's authority to transfer, reassign, abolish, or consolidate combatant functions of the armed forces. The National Security Act as being the prerogative of Congress had imposed such restrictions. This was a direct threat to the Marine Corps function. Commandant Randolph McCall Pate submitted a statement to the House Armed Service Committee as follows:

The Marine Corps is the only one of the services which is actually affected in any fundamental respect by this proposal to give over to the secretary of defense the present Congressional authority to abolish and transfer combatant functions. None of the other services is vitally concerned. I very much doubt if there is any real prospect of anyone wanting to take away from the Air Force the task you have given it—conducting warfare in the air: and the same goes for the Navy in the manner of naval warfare and the same for the Army regarding its important responsibilities for combat on land.

It is the Marine Corps alone-an organization brought into being to meet a strategic situation which is peculiar to this insular nation—an organization designed specifically for the short notice expeditionary tasks which have confronted us so often in the past and will exist in the future-that stands in jeopardy from this proposal. Witnesses from both sides made their case and Congress was not loathe to penetrate to the heart of the problem. The House Armed Service Committee made these comments:

* On the scope of activity of the office of the Secretary of Defense: It was never intended, and is not now intended, that the office of the Secretary of Defense would become a fourth department within the Department of Defense, delving into operational details on a daily basis.
* On the presidents desire to eliminate the requirement that the Defense Secretary deal with the military. If the military secretaries are to be something more than branch managers, they must be responsible for execution of the directives issued by the Secretary of Defense. If the requirement is eliminated, the separate identity of the services, the decentralization of the military departments would become a myth.
* On the president's desire to authorize the Secretary of Defense to reassign, abolish, or consolidate combatant functions of the armed services—an action prohibited by the National Security Act.

Congress must exercise its constitutional responsibility in this area. Such a grant of authority to the Executive Branch would constitute a complete surrender of Constitutional authority.

Despite misgivings, the vote proceeded along party lines and gave President Eisenhower much of what he asked for. President Eisenhower wanted this procedure changed and codified in law. This excluded the Joint Chiefs of Staff from any executive function in the assignment of military missions. These 1958 changes, although threatening to the Marine Corps, went far beyond Congress' responsibility. The sensitive balance achieved by the National Security Act was largely destroyed. The assurance that civilian matters related to defense would be handled by broad base of civilian officialdom was gone. The military departments and their secretaries were excluded from the decision making process and the President and Congress would receive one consolidated budget from the Secretary of Defense to the Joint Chiefs of Staff. This was a steady growth in the defense bureaucracy along with the expansion of the office of Secretary of Defense into professional military areas.

The trend has continued from Artemus Gates to the present Secretary of Defense, Leon Panetta who have undertaken to enlarge the scope of that office.

Like the other services, the Marine Corps has felt the burden of the massive Secretary of Defense superstructure but it has actually grown stronger since 1947.

The general order #5 triumph was another major event solidifying the Marine Corps position in the Department of the Navy.

A final step was taken in late 1978 when the Commandant of the Marine Corps was accorded full membership in the Joint Chiefs of Staff.

The Army was not alone in disrespecting the Marine Corps. The Navy's Bureau of Boats also had problems.

I will quote from FIRST TO FIGHT, beginning on page 71. The military world seems to be particularly prone to use cliché-thoughts and statements that do not bear the trial of proof. Classic among these is General Dwight D. Eisenhower's pronouncement in 1950 that "an amphibious landing is not a particularly difficult thing . . . You put your men in boats and as long as you get well trained crews to take the boats in, it is the simplest deployment in the world, the men can go nowhere else except the beach." As if getting to the beach was the whole game instead of just the beginning. Another classic is General Omar Bradley's untimely rumination, "I am wondering if we shall ever have another large scale amphibious operation." This, only 11 months before the dramatic amphibious assault by the First Marine Division and the first Marine Aircraft Wing at Inchon, Korea.

Also questionable is the frequently heard generalization that man has conducted amphibious attacks since the beginning of history. It is not altogether true. Man has indeed gone to war in ship, boats, or battle canoes since history began. He has undertaken innumerable expeditions overseas, using the ocean as a bridge to the enemy's homeland. From time to time, he has been able to put his forces ashore from the sea in the vicinity of the enemy's principal strength.

But a true amphibious assault against an opponent who has organized the beaches and the sea approaches for defense with entrenched infantry and an array of mutually supporting arms is quite another thing. And if the enemy is on an island or a peninsula, where the attacker is limited in his choice of landing site and where the crisis is likely to occur near the beachline, then it is even more difficult. The techniques for bringing off such an undertaking are a relatively modern development, going back in concept to only the 19th century.

Until the British landing at Gallipoli in 1915, the concept of an amphibious assault against determined resistance had little test, and the British violated so many basic principles that the test was deceptive.

The amphibious assault, at the Gallipoli, never taken too seriously, was largely discounted. Offshore mines, beach obstacles, heavy artillery in fortified emplacments, and integrated air defense.

The delay of landing by the British allowed the Ottoman officers to prepare defenses and allowed the Ottomans four good weeks to prepare. After the initial landing, not much advantage was taken of the situation, apart from a few tentative steps inland and most troops stayed on or not far from the beach. The Allied attack therefore lost momentum and the Ottomans had time to bring up reinforcements and rally the initial small number of defending troops.

Aircraft, for both observation and attack, were all seen as favoring the defense so much as to make such an assault "difficult, indeed almost impossible," according to British military historian B.H. Liddell Hart.

It is at this point that the Marines entered the historical scene. In truth, however, both before and after Gallipoli only a very few Marines were convinced of the feasibility of amphibious assault operations.

Very few visionaries were willing to attack the formidable conceptual, tactical and material problems associated with the modern amphibious assault landing. How to get heavy equipment and weapons ashore through surf and across reefs, how to exercise Command authority during the sensitive transition period, how to communicate effectively with ships and aircraft, how to cope with mines and beach obstacles, how to provide accurate, timely and concentrated fire support for the assault forces, how to ensure the essential supplies were delivered ashore where and when needed, how to manage the evacuation of casualties to seaward, and how to persuade the Navy to share its very limited resources in solving these problems.

Among these was John A. LeJeune, a compassionate gentleman, fearless fighter, a skilled diplomat, and a sensitive military thinker. He may not have been the first to say it, but no one of that era said it any better. With a prescience of a true pioneer, he declared in 1915 that the ability not just to defend, but to seize those bases was a logical and critical Marine function in light of the Navy's growing strategic responsibilities. He saw the Marine Corps as the first to set foot on hostile soil in order to seize, fortify and hold a base.

1st Lieutenant Earl H. Ellis was widely recognized as a brilliant planner both in the Navy and the Marines. He left behind a precious legacy in the form of an extraordinary 30,000 word study entitled: "Advanced Base Operations in Micronesia." It turned out to be an uncannily accurate forecast of things to Lieutenant Ellis outlined the step-by-step drive westward across the Pacific to meet the need as he saw it for bases to support the fleet, both during its projection and afterward. He traced the root to the Marshall and Caroline Islands much as it actually happened.

Contemporary with Ellis, and one of the few Marines who foresaw the future of amphibious warfare, was Dion Williams who served aboard the USS Baltimore under Admiral George Dewey at Manila Bay. Williams is credited with persuading Admiral Dewey to assert before the Congress that a force of 5,000 Marines with the fleet would have prevented the Philippine insurrection that ensued following the Spanish defeat. From 1899 to 1902, William's concept of such a "force" was probably the first tiny beginning of the doctrinal sequence that became the "base defense force," The Expeditionary Force and, finally, the "Fleet Marine Force."

In 1933, General Douglas MacArthur, who was Chief of Staff of the Army and openly antagonistic to the Marine Corps on the grounds that the Marine Corps constituted an economic affront to the Army, proposed to the President, and to several members of Congress, that the Marines, air and ground, be transferred to the Army.

Failing in that proposal, MacArthur then proposed that the bulk of the Marine Corps be transferred to the Army, leaving Marines with only base defense and seagoing functions.

The substantial influence wielded by Douglas MacArthur as Chief of Staff of the Army impressed Marine Commandant Ben H. Fuller with the gravity of the threat, and gave his assistant, General Russell the opportunity to drive to the surface the amphibious subject. He persuaded the Commandant that a formalized, written body of amphibious doctrine was needed, and it should be prepared by the Marines themselves. It should be in great detail and should exhibit that they possessed a unique capability not shared by anyone, particularly the Army. In charge of the project was Brigadier General James C. Breckinridge, but the driving force was Colonel Ellis B. Miller. He produced the tentative manual for landing operations. Miller was not content with the manual and the Corps set immediately to revise, update, and perfect the manual. The manual was ground breaking of the purist sort and the Navy adopted it as Fleet Training Publication no.167, "landing operation doctrine, U.S. Navy." Three years later, in 1941, the Army, whose interest in amphibious operations had been minimal, copied the manual, lock, stock, and barrel, and published it as "field marshal 31-5."

# IDEAS BUT NO BOATS

The innovative brilliance of those Marines who nourished the idea of the amphibious assault is in no way dimmed by the fact that their wonderful dream would not have become a reality had it not been for an unusual man named Andy Higgins. He was living proof of the adage "one man with courage is a majority."

Since 1933, only a half dozen crafts were tried but none came close to what the Marines needed for amphibious warfare. In the next ten years, nothing happened in the resource-starved Navy to move the ship to shore operation from an idea to a reality. Nevertheless, the Marines at headquarters in Washington kept pressure on the Navy to somehow find funds to get the heavy weapons into the battle.

The first break came in September of 1937, Victor Krulak was a Lieutenant serving as assistant intelligence officer in the 4th Marines in Shanghai at the time fighting erupted between the Chinese and Japanese. He got permission, first from the Marines, then from the Navy, and then from the Japanese, to observe a Japanese amphibious assault on Chinese positions defending the Liuho area, at the mouth of the

Yangtze River. Victor Krulak was fortunate to fall in with George R. Phelan, USNA 25, the Assistant Fleet Intelligence Officer who was enthusiastic about my idea of seeing the war at close hand. He arranged a U.S. Navy tug for our transportation and the services of a Navy photographer's mate. The Japanese paid us little attention. We watched troops debarking into boats from transports. We watched destroyers deliver Naval gunfire on the beach prior to landing and in support of the advancing troops afterwards.

Most important, we got near enough to take close-up photographs of the Japanese assault landing craft. And there we saw in action exactly what the Marines had been looking for, a sturdy ramp bow-type boats capable of transporting heavy vehicles and depositing them directly on the beaches. What we saw was that the Japanese were light years ahead of us in landing-craft design.

Victor Krulak was excited about what he had seen and wrote an enthusiastic report on the various landing craft types the Japanese were using. The report, complete with photographs and sketches went off to Washington and he was confident that we would soon see a profusion of equally useful American ramp-bow landing craft.

After two years, in July 1939, upon returning to the United States he spent the day hunting for his report in the files of the Navy's Bureau of Ships. Finally unearthed, he was chagrined to read a marginal comment from some Bureau skeptic that the report was the work of "some nut out in China." Somewhat crestfallen, he nevertheless built a foot-long model of the boat similar to those he had seen in China and took it along with his 1937 China Report to Brigadier General H. M. Smith. He was excited about it and took the model and me to Washington and showed it to Commandant Holcomb. The Commandant was equally interested and said he would like to keep the boat and his report to show the Secretary of the Navy. He would be proud to say that this model was the stimulus for the beginning of the modern American landing craft program. Maybe it was, but the truth is that Victor Klrulak never saw or heard of the model again.

There was some activity in the landing field area. They tested a 50-foot motor launch to carry a heavy vehicle or a light tractor. In a test with no more than one or two feet of surf, the way the loaded boat rolled was so terrifying that the test was cancelled. The Navy built a one self-propelled tank carrying lighter boat of its own design in 1938, and two more in 1939, all capable of carrying a sixteen ton tank. All were underpowered and it was a serious problem in the surf. One of them overturned in the 1940 maneuvers.

Finally Brigadier General E.P. Moses and Major E.E.Linsert of the Marine Corps equipment board met Andrew Jackson Higgins of New Orleans.

In 1924, Higgins designed a powerful shallow draft thirty-six foot boat with a novel underwater hull, for use by Rum Runners in the Mississippi Delta, during prohibition. The design was ideal for beach landings because it protected the propeller from striking the bottom and facilitated retraction from the beach. He offered this boat called the "Eureka" to the Navy in 1926 and every year thereafter to meet the need for a landing craft to carry personnel and light equipment.

The Marines saw the Eureka for the first time in 1934 and perceived it to be a big step toward what they were seeking. They quickly formed a pact with Higgins, an alliance fertilized by their mutual impatience with the Navy Bureau of Ships for what they saw as its dilatory approach to the landing craft problem. Pressure generated by the alliance resulted in the Navy reluctantly purchased one of the boats.

It was tested in conjunction with three Bureau of Ships designed boats in a 1939 exercise in the Caribbean but, despite great Marine enthusiast, it received only qualified approval. Five more Eureka boats were purchased in time to take part, along with twelve Bureau of Ships designed boats in a major amphibious exercise in the Caribbean in 1940, where the Higgins boats performed extremely well. With war on the horizon, Major General Holland M. Smith, in command of the Marines in the exercise assessed the boat situation with his usual candor. He said that the field test of the Bureau of Ships designed boats disclosed them to be "without merit." If we had 300 of the Higgins boats and the ships to carry them, we would be in business.

In March of 1941, General Smith sent Klulak to New Orleans along with Major Linsert of the Equipment Board to explain our needs. First, they asked Higgins to redesign his Eureka boat to incorporate a ramp for landing small vehicles. Krulak showed the pictures of the Japanese craft in Shanghai in 1937 and the picture of the model he had made in 1939. Secondly, they asked him to design a steel tank carrying a lighter boat capable of carrying an eighteen ton tank.

Higgins took both ideas aboard at once and proceeded at his own expense to rebuild two of his Eureka boats from 30 to 36 feet to incorporate a bow ramp. In the space of 61 hours, he quickly converted a 45 foot steel lighter boat which he had built for the Columbia Government, into a ramp bow craft capable of carrying an eighteen ton tank.

Both ideas worked. The Marines were ecstatic. The Navy however, was more hesitant, opting to buy only five more of the Higgins thirty-six foot ramp type boats for further testing and evaluation. This time the evaluation was conducted by a board of Marine

Corps, and Navy officers. The board's report was overwhelmingly favorable. The Navy then ordered two hundred of the Higgins ramp type boats and the Landing Craft Vehicle and Personnel were a reality.

The Bureau of Ships declined to invest any money in a Higgins designed tank carrying lighter, since they had a design for a steel tank carrier of their own, despite unfavorable reports that they were slow, difficult to control, difficult to retract and equipped with an unpredictable power plant. The Bureau had awarded the first increment of 1,100 units to another company the previous six months. Delivery of the tank carrying lighters was six months behind schedule, and none would be available for the exercise. The need for a tank carrier was so great that General Smith persuaded the Bureau of Ships to order one of the craft from Higgins. It was a success resulting in an order for nine more. Higgins managed to turn out the nine lighters in twelve days and ship them off by rail to Norfolk for the maneuvers.

The craft was a huge success but Higgins still got no more orders. The American Car and Foundry Co. (ACF), who had the contract for 96 of the 1,100 crafts and the Bureau explained that the craft designed by the Bureau would be superior to the Higgins product because the tanks would be carried above the water line and could not be swamped. In the Higgins craft, the tank rode below the waterline, making the boat more stable.

All of this was too much for Higgins and his impatient Marine friends. They went at once to powerful Senator Harry Truman, Chairman of the Senate Committee on Preparedness. Influenced by their story and by two meetings with Higgins, the Senator laid a hard demand on the Navy, "produce one of your boats, put it in a head to head test with the Higgins product and see what happens."

By early March of 1942, the ACF tank carrier of the Bureau of Ships with its enlarged design to handle the Army's thirty-ton Army tank made its appearance. Higgins also enlarged his tank carrier to handle the tank for the competition.

Everyone was there, the senior representatives from the Navy Department, the Bureau of Ships, the Marine Corps, as well as the Army, which were greatly interested because of emerging plans for the North African amphibious landing. The Marines also brought an administrative assistance from Senator Truman's office.

Both boats, loaded with thirty tons of dead weight, came around the corner side by side and, as they turned south heading for the beach, the trouble began. Caught in the trough of the big ocean swells, the Bureau of Ships designed craft with its higher center of gravity, began to roll. It rolled more and more until everyone feared it might capsize. The coxswain, realizing that it was in danger, cut back its power and after wallowing uncertainly for a few moments, turned slowly around and headed back for shelter.

The contest was over. The Higgins craft drove ahead through the rough seas, landed handily through the heavy surf, and retracted without difficulty. Then, almost as an act of defiance, it did it twice more. The Marine dreams of the true amphibious assault became a reality.

For the first time, there was a reliable way to make tanks, trucks, tractors, artillery, anti-aircraft weapons, and heavy engineer equipment, a part of the beach assault.

Thenceforward, America's amphibious march across the Pacific would be, as far as boats were concerned, Andy Higgins' war. A tribute to Higgins it certainly is. Equally, it is testimonial to the persistence of the Marine Corps of three generations, a fact that Higgins understood. He wrote to General Smith. "My contact with the Marine Corps is my bright spot of my recollection of those intense and hectic days. I believe the things we foresaw and did had a profound effect on winning the war."

Why all of this poison atmosphere against the Marine Corps? I would have to say that it all began during World War I, when General John Pershing did not like the Marines and their motto "First to fight." Quoting from the book **BRUTE**, the life of Victor Krulak, U.S Marine, by Robert Coram, I will glean and paraphrase from this book and all of the books that I will quote from and will not change the meaning of what was written.

General John Pershing was to make the fighting in Europe an all Army affair. But if the Marines were not part of the fighting, they would probability not be of any worthwhile fighting unit and would almost certainly be disbanded. The Commandant of the Marine Corps George Barnett went over General Pershing's head to the Secretary of War, Newton D. Baker who sent two Marine Regiments to France. They formed the 4th Brigade with fewer than 8,000 men.

General Pershing did not like the Marines and was offended by their "First to Fight" motto. Marines were not alone in being prevented from doing their jobs by Pershing. His headquarters would not allow American war correspondents near the front, and when American forces went into battle they could not identify, by name, any of the Army regiments and could not distinguish between regular troops and National Guard or between infantry and artillery. They could report only that units or elements of the Army were in combat. Little did he know that he had condemned the Army to anonymity.

Several stories exist as to how correspondents were able to use the word "Marines" in their dispatches. They argued that since they could use the word "Army" they should be able to write of "Marines." Censors agreed, overlooking the fact that there was only one brigade of Marines in France and that simply saying "Marines" was the same as using a unit designation. In a very short time, Pershing's decision would explode in ways he never anticipated and would forever regret.

In the spring of 1918, the Americans were going into battle against the unstoppable German Army, and everywhere, the question was asked, "Can the Americans fight?"

The American correspondents were ecstatic that the Americans were moving into the line of combat. Most Journalists attached themselves to Army units, but Floyd Gibbons, a correspondent from the Chicago Tribune, decided that he would go over the top with the Marines. Many Marines were now wearing the same Khaki Uniforms as the Army. Marine officers also wore the Marine insignia—the eagle globe and anchor on their helmets and collars. By now, the Marines accounted for less than one percent of the American Expeditionary force (AEF) and were described by an

Army historian as "that little raft of sea soldiers in an ocean of Army." But they were proud and a cocky bunch and Gibbons liked that.

Quoting from the book, **THE DEVIL DOGS AT BELLEAU WOODS** by Dick Camp. When President Woodrow Wilson announced that the United States had declared war on Germany, war fever gripped the country. Young men streamed to the colors. Many were then on their way to Parris Island, an insect-infested spit of swampland off the coast of Port Royal, South Carolina. It was an isolated outpost covered with stunted scrub pine, a wind-blown, sandy land. Upon arrival, the recruits were turned over to NCO's who quickly introduced them to their hardcore training methods. One recruit wrote, "The first day at camp I thought I was going to die." After the training at Parris Island, including two weeks at the rifle range, the men were transferred to the overseas depot at Quantico, Virginia, for advanced training before shipping off to France. Despite a shortage of trained men, the Army did not want Marines and dredged up phony roadblocks, which in the cold light of day proved to be groundless.

Marine Commandant Major General George Barnett enlisted the aid of President Woodrow Wilson who ordered the Secretary of War and directed him to issue the necessary orders detaching for service with the Army a force of Marines to be known as the 5th

Regiment of Marines. The Secretary penned a note to General Barnett with one last ploy, "I am sorry to have to tell you that it will be utterly impossible for the War Department to furnish transportation for a Marine Regiment with the first outfit sailing.

General Barnett had an ace up his sleeve, a friend and ally, Admiral W. S. Benson, Chief of Naval Operation, had reserved three naval transports for the Marines. General Barnett wrote to Secretary Baker "Please give yourself no further trouble in this matter, as transportation has been arranged."

The transport, U.S.S. Hancock arrived on June 13 and began embarking troops and equipment and sailed, but instead to France it found itself in New York harbor. To add insult to injury, the USS Hancock was too slow and another Ship, the U.S.S. Henderson was substituted and remained at anchor for several days,

On June 26, 1917, the DeKalb finally arrived at the harbor of St. Nazaire. The Henderson with the remainder of the 5th Marines arrived the next day. The Marines stayed aboard ship for several days waiting for orders. They were dismayed to learn that the regiment was not to be kept intact. One battalion in St. Nazaire, half a battalion in England and one battalion a few miles from Menaucourt. "First to fight" was changed to first to work. Marines found themselves on work parties as guards and the most hated assignment as military police. But they did their duty. The second battalion, 5th Marines were ordered to a training area at Gondrecourt by train with those famous "40 & 8" box cars, which meant 40 men and 8 horses. It had recently transported horses because it smelled like a horse barn. After one day's travel, they detrained at Menaucouet. The Marines were trained by the French veterans, "Blue Devils" in trench warfare, they considered themselves a corps d'elite and were proud of their war record.

The Marines dug a series of trenches, took up the new method of bayonet fighting and were put through a gas chamber. The threat of gas was very real. In the early morning of April 13, a German artillery barrage lasting more than 4 hours struck the 1st battalion, 6th Marines. Of the estimated 3000 shells, 1800 were gas.

The French and British officers were snobs. They felt that we should have been put under their commands. The American troops would have been if it had not been that General Pershing who held out and insisted that all American troops were to be under our command.

Quoting again from the book <u>BRUTE,</u> General Pershing did not like the Marines. On St. Patrick's Day, the Marines moved out and relieved a French battalion in the line. They moved forward and entered into one of the trenches, mud caked shoes made it difficult to walk in the slime and it would stick to the uniform and the equipment. The dugout was infested with rats, huge rats, not field mice. The Marines had to shoot them. On April 6, the battle heated up and several contacts with the Germans were made with a number of Marines wounded and killed.

The Germans realized that there was a new outfit in front of them and they wanted to capture prisoners to determine who we were. The Marines settled into a routine of raids, night patrols and artillery barrages. In early May, after fifty-three days in the Line, the Marine Brigade was relieved and rejoined the 2nd division for final training. On May 27, a massive German offensive smashed through the French and British lines, unnerving the British and French high command. The Germans made a salient that ran down the Marne River and that was a straight dash into Paris. All they had to do was to go another twenty-five miles. The attack seemed unstoppable. Another 24 hours and the French would be out of the war.

There were not enough reserves to plug the gap. A hurried call went out to the inexperienced American 2nd division: "March to the sound of the guns." A French General, worried that the Americans could not hold. Colonel Preston Brown, the 2nd Division Chief of Staff, replied "General, these are American regulars. In 150 years they have never been beaten. They will hold," The 4th Marine Brigade was ordered up to the front and as they rode in French army trucks, they were not comfortable at all.

The men traveled 14 miles, skirting Paris, and headed toward the front. Late on the afternoon of June 1, the lead elements of the Brigade reached its destination on the Paris-Metz road, nine miles north of Chateau Thierry. The Germans had advanced from artillery sound to machine gun sound. They were coming and they were moving fast toward Paris. A French officer was trying to convince the American Commander to fall back. The American Commander retorted "I have come to fight Germans and this is here I intend to do it, and that is that." They were ordered to form a defensive line from the northeast corner of Veuilly Wood. You have to get there right away. The Marines don't expect the French to stick and the Germans may get there before we do. When they got there, there was no one on their right side. His 1,000 Marines faced the German onslaught alone. Remnants of French units passed through their lines in full retreat. They cried, "Turn back, the war is over, the Germans are victorious." One haggard French officer buttonholed Captain Williams and gestured toward the rear ordered Captain Williams to retreat. Williams replied, "Retreat hell, we just got here" Captain Williams sent a message to the Battalion Commander. The French Major gave me a written order to fall back. I have countermanded his order, kindly see that the French do not shorten their artillery and shell us.

# The following six photos were from the book Devil Dogs at BelleauWood

The Americans stood tall, eager to prove themselves to the Boche and avenge the atrocities the Germans were alleged to have committed. *Charles Baldridge—National Museum of the Marine Corps*

When Captain William's men were in position, we witnessed the German advance. It was an arrow aimed directly at Les Mares Farm. It was a key position as we realized and all we had was a thin red line of Marines with a man about every ten feet apart. A Marine with a rifle, but we held our lines." German infantry advanced five hundred yards-four, three until the trained riflemen waited the order to fire. When they fired, the Germans staggered and fell. The deadly accurate rifle fire stopped the attackers in their track. They fell by scores among the wheat and the poppies. The Germans who had thoroughly trounced the French thought that it was a cakewalk to Paris. The Marines fought on and captured hill #142 which the Germans really wanted. The Germans launched several attacks in a short time and failed.

Their next objective was the village of Bouresches and the railroad station. The Marines moved out in wave formation. The Marines advanced down a slope to a field covered with waist high wheat. All was quiet until the Marines were within range. The Germans opened up with their machine guns and artillery fire. Machine gun fire from Belleau Woods was taking its toll. The Marines entered the western part of the town and began a house to house fight. The Germans had three to four hundred men in the town. They had machine guns at street corners, behind barricades and even barricades on house tops.

GO OVER THE TOP WITH

U.S. MARINES

ds of dramatic recruiting and home-front posters produced to inspire patriotism decorated homes and p
lings throughout the country. This poster, "Over the Top," used a term first coined by the British to signi
attacking out of their trenches. *Marine Corps History Division*

But the Marines kept on. They attacked with rifles, bayonets and grenades. They were outnumbered when they started, but one by one they kept going, taking gun after gun until the Germans began to fall back. The Germans still held the railroad station. On June 13, James Harbord reported that there was only Marines in the town. The attack on Bouresches cost hundreds of Marine casualties but the casualties were worth it. If we had not gotten Bouresches, we would not have a chance in Belleau Wood. The next objective was Belleau Wood.

According to Marine historian Robert Debs Heinl, Belleau Wood was a carefully organized center of resistance held by 1200 Germans, the largest single body of combat-seasoned regular troops which the Marines had to confront. The Germans had set up machine guns and large mortars, turning the Belleau Wood into one huge machine gun nest containing two hundred of these weapons. At 5:00 pm the officers whistles sounded and the Marines went forward.

The dashing reckless Chicago Tribune correspondent, Floyd Gibbons, received permission to accompany the attack. The field was perfectly flat and covered with a young crop of oats between ten to fifteen inches high. The field was bordered on both sides by dense cluster of trees where Germans had machine guns.

Before the attack, Gibbons sent a dispatch to the Chicago Tribune "I am up front with the U.S. Marines." The New York Times picked up the story "Our Marines attack gain miles, and resume drive at night—foes losing heavily. "The Chicago Daily Tribune screamed, "Marines win hot battle, sweep enemy from Heights near Thierry."

The accounts were the first that mentioned specific units of the Army by name and it made it appear that the Marines were winning the war all by themselves. The Army was not amused and was convinced that the Leathernecks were a corps of publicity hounds. According to the book BRUTE, Pershing realized his mistake and forbid correspondents to mention Marines in any future dispatches. But it was too late. America had begun its love affair with the Marines.

Continuing from The book THE DEVIL DOGS at BELLEAU WOOD, Second Lieutenant William A. Eddy, an intelligence officer of the 6th Marines, and his two scouts, lay concealed in the uncut field. The crunch of hob-nail boots, guttural commands and the muffled sound of engineer tools drowned out the night sounds. They reported, "the Germans are organizing in the woods and consolidating their machine gun positions." Except for Eddy's brief foray, the Marine Brigade was going into the attack with precious little intelligence. Maps were scarce and the contours gave no real information as to the physical features of the ground. A messenger arrived with orders for the 3rd Battalion, 6th Marines, to seize the southern lobe of the woods. When Nevelle asked about artillery support, he was told that it was not planned for because there was no need of it. An observer from the French Escadron 252 (aircraft squadron) had earlier reported that the sector was calm. A 2nd Division unpublished report stated, "At 5:00 P.M. the officers whistles shrilled. And the two Battalions of Marines went forward. The lines were carefully dressed in the four-wave platoon formation. They proceeded across the field which was perfectly flat and covered with a young crop of oats. The German machine guns opened fire and hammered away at the exposed Marines. They hadn't gotten across the field before the first line of survivors had merged with the second. There was no cover in the open wheat field for four hundred yards or more and they were shot to pieces, ending the attack almost before it had begun.

The shrill notes of officers' whistles sounded along the battalion front. A thousand Marines deployed into formation in a two company front about nine hundred meters wide. The two left flank companies advanced quickly through the southern end of the woods against light opposition and gained a height that was unoccupied. Suddenly they ran into the main German defenders and were stopped cold. Immediately, a terrible fire opened up from the left flank and from our left rise of ground about fifty yards away from the German machine guns. There were machine guns everywhere. The losses were staggering. More Marines had been killed and wounded in action than in the 143 years of the Corps' history. The battalion was deployed on the ridge facing Belleau Wood. The Germans pounded the position with a continuous shelling and unceasing stream of machine gun and rifle fire. The battalion absorbed tremendous punishment for the next three days. Orders came to attack from the southern edge of the woods into the teeth of the German defenses. According to an unpublished account, "The weight of the German defense lay southward, exactly where the Marine attack struck the German line." The Germans had positioned light machine guns to cover every path and clearing. Heavy machine guns protected by swarms of infantry, backed them up, creating a near perfect defense. The French told the Americans that the woods were not strongly held. The whistles sounded and the Marine battalion rose to its feet. Fixed bayonets, and rifles at the ready, they started their slow advance. The forest loomed ahead, dark and foreboding. Suddenly a crackling sheath of machine gun fire encased our battalion, closing in on us fiercely. Many hurled themselves into the nearest shell hole, but a few of them pushed forward until their legs were shot out from under them. Other Marines spotted a machine gun. They charged it. Two were killed but the rest surrounded the gun crew, who wanted to surrender. There is not much use in taking prisoners of men who fire at you until they see that they are overpowered. I don't remember any prisoners walking back from that crowd. Some of the men were advancing and disappeared into the woods. You could hear the sounds of fighting. The detonations of the barrage had ceased. A sudden burst of machine gun fire would break out, which meant that the Marines were advancing on a nest. It would die down which meant that the nest was taken. Foot by foot they had pushed through the underbrush in the face of continuous machine gun and rifle fire. As the wounded were being carried back passing an open space, the German machine gun sniper would pick off the wounded. Two of the German companies were overrun and simply disappeared. Two other companies were forced out of position and retreated toward the Northeast.

A German soldier wrote "My company has been reduced from 120 to 30 men, We had Americans opposite us who are terribly reckless fellows." The following morning, the exhausted survivors went forward and almost immediately they ran into intense German fire.

Dozens were cut down as the Marines advanced across the open ground. German machine-gun fire was unmerciful— men were hit and hit again as they fell. *John W. Thomason, Jr., Fix Bayonets!*

Casualties mounted. Officers went down and Sergeants took over and when they went down Corporals took over and when they went down Privates took over. In the mist of the carnage, a Marine yelled "Eyah." The battle cry he had learned at boot camp. The yell they had learned on the bayonet course, sticking dummies and, in that narrow neck of Belleau Wood, it was taken up and shouted savagely. The Marines were startled by that yell. Fear, hunger and fatigue were forgotten in a mad lust to ram two feet of steel into some German soldiers. The Marines pressed forward, overrunning the enemy's advance position, breaking through their main line of heavy machine guns. As the Marines reached the edge of the woods near hill 133, a group of gray clad figures got up like a covey of frightened quail, big husky Germans running over the plowed ground in their heavy boots. A wounded English speaking German officer stepped out of the underbrush and hailed a Marine officer. A number of enemy soldiers watched from the woods. The men trained their rifles at the newcomers in a tense standoff. The Marine officer recovered quickly and offered the German a cigarette. The German asked for a guide to take him and his men back to surrender. Forty-two Germans with a small detail of guards followed them into captivity.

"Marines at Belleau Wood: U.S. Marines cleaning out machine-gun nests in Belleau Wood."
*Frank E. Schoonover–National Museum of the Marine Corps*

The stone Pavillon was the French landlord's hunting lodge. The area around it was heavily defended and had to be taken by the bayonet. *George Scott—Cold Steel, U.S. Marines First Hand Battle, eyewitness—The Chicago Daily News War Postal Card Department*

The Marines were so exhausted after two weeks of battle with little sleep and no hot food, subsiding on iron rations and very little water. Heavy casualties approaching 50 percent had greatly reduced combat efficiency. The Commanding Officer requested the use of the 7th Infantry to relieve the Brigade.

The 7th Infantry held the line for the Marines from June 15 to June 24, enabling the Brigade to rest and recuperate. On the 23rd of June, the 3rd Battalion, 5th Marines, were ordered back with orders to clear the woods forthwith. The Battalion went over the top and ran into the same buzz saw of German machine gun positions. The attack failed. The concentration of heavy machine guns could not be wiped out by infantry. It was decided to pound the German positions with artillery. Seven hundred Marines went over this time, all that was left of the Battalion. They had only gone a little distance when the Germans opened up with two-pounders causing many casualties. Reaching the top of a little knoll, the Germans opened up with machine guns, hand and rifle grenades and mortars. Just then we all seemed to go crazy for we gave a yell like a bunch of wild Indians and started down the hill running and cursing in the face of machine gun fire. Men were falling but they continued, yelling and firing as they went. The fight continued into the night. The 47th Company was being counter attacked and needed artillery support. U.S. Marine Corps were entirely alone and the Question "Can these Americans fight?" was answered.

The Marines, along with the 2nd Army Division, so damaged the German army that after Belleau Wood five German divisions were declared unfit for further combat.

In 1918, Belleau Wood would be the closest the German Army got to Paris.

Quoting again from the book <u>BRUTE</u>: On June 30, the French high command, over the objections of Pershing, sent out word that in all official papers Bois de Belleau henceforth be known as Bois de la Brigade de Marine. As far as the French were concerned it was the Marines who had saved the City of Lights. They were awarded the Croix de Guerre and today the 5th and 6th Regiments still wear a branded green and red rope called a fourragere on their left shoulder, a quiet announcement that their professional antecedents fought at Belleau Wood.

On July 10, President Wilson reported to the U.S. Senate that the Marines had turned the tide of battle and that Belleau Wood had begun the rout that was to save the world. One writer described the Western front as a great rubber band that had been stretched to its limit and now snapped back toward Germany.

With the example of the U. S Marines before them, the Allies had seized the initiative. The German Army was in retreat. The end of the war was obvious.

In November, the Armistice was signed. By then, the Marine Brigade had taken about 4000 casualties, some 55 percent of its original strength and of any American Brigade in World War I. Many of the Marines who died at Belleau Wood were later taken home for reburial, but more than 300 are buried there in the Aisne-Marne American Cemetery, an out of the way place of France that is forever American. After the war, however the Army-dominated Battle Monument Commission would not allow the Marine Corps emblem to be placed in the cemetery, nor would the Army allow a statue of a Marine or marker to be erected to acknowledge this place as the Bois de la Brigade de Marine. However the Battle Monument Commission built a Memorial near Chateau Therry to commemorate the sacrifices and achievements of the American and French soldiers. After Belleau Wood, the Marines were no longer a small, shipborne gendarmere. They had entered the world of massed firepower, and in future wars they would demonstrate that they could respond with more trained and equipped combat troops quicker than any other branch of the U.S. Military. Not only would their boots be the first on the ground in America's future wars, but the word "Marine" would become synonymous with the word "victory"

If the Marines could win at Belleau Wood, it was now expected that they could win anywhere. In 1997, General Lemuel Shepherd, Commandant of the Marine Corps went to Belleau Wood to videotape a message to all Marines upon the occasion of the 222nd birthday of the Marine Corps.

He ended a powerful and emotional address by putting the events at Belleau Wood as a great river that runs through the heart of every Marine. One of the things for which Lemuel Shepherd is revered in the Marine Corps is that as Commandant, he redressed a great wrong. He visited Belleau Wood and found that there was still no marker showing that the Marines had fought there, no marker showing that Belleau Wood had been renamed the Bois de la Brigade de Marine and no marker saying that Marines were buried there. The American Battle Monuments Commission continued to refuse even the use of a Marine Corps Emblem in the cemetery. Commandant Shepherd changed that, adding a striking bas relief in Bronze on a black granite slab that still stands today at Belleau Wood. The inscription reads, "May the gallant Marines who gave their lives for Corps and Country rest in peace." Underneath the inscription is the Eagle, Globe and Anchor.

# PRESIDENTS & ARMY GENERALS

General Pershing was a Commander of the AEF in World War I and was not in love with the Marine Corps, as was written in the book <u>Devil Dogs at Belleau Wood</u>.

General Mathew B. Ridgeway looked back on Belleau Wood and stated that it was a prime example of men being thrown away.

Dwight D. Eisenhower was a Lieutenant in World War I and became a President of the United States who tried to downsize or eliminate the Marine Corps as a whole as was also written in above books.

Harry S. Truman was a Captain in the Army Artillery in World War I and also became a President of the United States who also tried to downsize or eliminate the Marine Corps as a whole. Stating" The Marine Corps is the Navy's police force, and as long as I am president, that is what it will remain." Why all this animosity against the Marines?

Douglas MacArthur was promoted to 1st Lieutenant in 1914 and to Major in 1915 and entered the World

War I as a Major and was decorated for his distinguish service achievement on the battlefield. He received 7 Silver Stars and the distinguish Service Cross. **7 Silver Stars**?

According to the book <u>AMERICAN CAESAR</u> by William Manchester, when General Pershing ordered 33 of the Rainbows Division to other units, MacArthur went to Pershing headquarters to protest, but his objection was ignored. Censorship not yet been imposed. MacArthur sent cables to Washington and Senators and Congressmen of influence from states representing the Rainbow Division asking them to demand that the Rainbow Division, be kept intact. General Pershing finally relented. In MacArthur's memoirs, he conceded that his politicking was probably in strict accord with normal procedure. He came to believe that people in the Army were out to get him, and the desk bound men envied a fighting officer. He lumped them all together with the Awards Board that had rejected his candidacy for the Medal of Honor. This was the beginning of his paranoia that was to bring so much anguish to him and others in the years ahead.

The antagonism between George C. Marshal and Lt. Colonel Douglas MacArther would grow with grave consequences for the country. During this time, he was promoted to Colonel and placed in charge of the Rainbow Division.

MacArthur's legend was growing. He refused to carry a gas mask and was gassed on March 11. His mother, the widow of the famous Major General Arthur MacArthur, wrote to General Pershing wondering why her 38 year old son was only a Colonel. Officers with AEF headquarters thought that MacArthur made too much of his name and called him "the show off."

MacArthur's mother was his ardent supporter, she had begun her campaign for his promotion, writing to Secretary of War Newton D. Baker stating "I am taking the liberty of addressing you on a matter close to my heart and in behalf of my son Douglas. I am deeply anxious to have Colonel MacArthur considered for the rank of Brigadier General. And it is only through you that he ever hopes to get this advancement." Secretary Baker did not reply but she was not discouraged. More letters followed stating that her heart's great wish was that he might see his way clear to bestow a star upon her son Douglas. Senator Baker wrote her and said that recommendations for promotions of all kind would come from General Pershing. She wrote to General Pershing again stating her late husband's admiration for him and understood that there would be 100 new appointments to general officers. "I know the Secretary of War and his family quite intimately and that the Secretary is very deeply attached to Colonel MacArthur and knows him quite well and I know that if my son is on your list for recommendation to a

Brigadier General that he would get the promotion." All the least attractive threat of mother and son were in these exchanges: the servility, the self-seeking, the flattery and naked threats of intercession by high authority. MacArthur became the youngest Brigadier General in the Army at the age of 38.

Sergeant Alexander Woolcott, wrote in the Stars and Stripes: "The Boche rear guard were driven back to the hills of Belgium and Luxemburg. The Rainbow Division joined the battle on November 4, when it relieved the 78th Division 12 miles south of Sedan.

Everybody wanted to take Sedan. Militarily it was insignificant, invested with glamour. General Pershing was determined to reach it before the French who was advancing on the left.

MacArthur, though was unaware that the U. S. troops were about to attack across his front, he had grave doubts about the Rainbow Division advancing before dawn. He suggested a delay until dawn. That gave him greater promise of success than one would make at night, and it was agreed to.

MacArthur had retired to his bed when word reached him that strange troops were swarming in his area. A 16th infantry patrol led by Lieutenant Black coming upon an officer leaning over a map and wearing a floppy hat, muffler, riding breaches and polished boots, assumed that he must be a German Officer. MacArthur was taken prisoner at pistol point and was then released with apologies. His troops could have captured Sedan in the morning but they were relieved in the general muddle.

MacArthur was awarded his 7th Silver Star for gallantry in the capture of the Meuse Heights and was promoted to Corps Commander. At 38, he was the youngest Division Commander of the war.

General Pershing had recommended him for Major General but the war ended and all promotions were frozen.

With all his accomplishments, he became a controversy with people who knew him. William Manchester wrote that Americans above a certain age hold strong opinions about Douglas MacArthur. They either worship him or despise him, and they are all wrong because their premises are rooted in apocrypha. Very few people really know Douglas MacArthur. Those who know him either admire him or dislike him. They are never neutral on the subject. No other American Commander has been more controversial. Harry Truman branded him as a counterfeit. Liberals and intellectuals denounced him as a Swashbuckler and a ham.

In spite of his 13 decorations his G.I's scorned him as "Dugout Doug."

In the book <u>BRUTE</u>, it is recorded that MacArthur fled aboard a P.T. Boat on March 11, 1942. He ordered citations and awards for the Army units that stayed behind to fight the invading Japanese. Then he struck the Marines from the list of recipients, saying, according to William Manchester in the book, <u>American Caesar, Douglas MacArthur 1880-1964</u>. MacArthur stated "The Marines had enough glory in World War I." He reiterated the same answer when he met with President Roosevelt, that he was only putting in the awards for Army troops. When Roosevelt asked him about the Marines, he answered the same line "They had their glory in World War I."

After World War II, many stories were written about Douglas MacArthur. Many believed that he was the greatest hero of World War II, but after reading many accounts and blunders in his career, I find it amazing how this so called grand hero was glamorized by the media. Of course all the publicity was provided by MacArthur himself.

Quoting from the book <u>WITH THE OLD BREED</u> by E. B. Sledge, World War II historians and military analysts have argued about the necessity of the Peleliu campaign.

Many believed after the battle, and still believe today, that the United States did not need to fight it as a prerequisite to MacArthur's return to the Philippine. It was his fearful concern about his right flank. He with the Joint Chiefs of Staff, ordered that the Marines invade Peleliu to give MacArthur an air base in order to bomb the Japanese on Mindanao. The taking of Peleliu cost the Marines 1,252 killed and 5,274 wounded. The real tragedy of Peleliu was that the landing was a battle that was rendered unnecessary almost before it began. Among the Senior Commanders, only Admiral Halsey had raised any doubts as to the necessity of taking Peleliu but his concerns were not heeded. When MacArthur sped up his taking of the Philippines and bypassed Mindinao for the landing at Leyte, the airfield at Peleliu for which so many died became obsolete.

Admiral William Halsey suggested the Peleliu operation be called off after high level planners learned that the Japanese air power in the Philippines was not as strong as intelligence originally had presumed it to be, but MacArthur believed that the operation should proceed, and Admiral Chester Nimitz said it was too late to cancel the operation because the convoy was already on its way.

Because of important events in Europe at the time and the lack of immediate, apparent benefits from the seizure of Peleliu, the battle remains one of the lesser known or understood of the Pacific war. Nonetheless, for many it ranks as the roughest fight the Marines had in World War II.

The handling of the Korean War was another mismanagement of his tenure. Quoting from the book, FOR COUNTRY and CORPS, the life of General Olive P Smith by Gail Shisler. After the Marine landing at Inchon, the recapture of Seoul was MacArthur's main focus. In his typically dramatic fashion, he wished for this event take place by 25 September, three months to the day from the city's capture by the North Koreans. The man who waded ashore in the Philippines, (that is four times until the right picture was acceptable to him, because the first picture showed him upset because he had to wade ashore in his pressed uniform instead of landing at the pier. After reviewing the first picture, he thought it made him more of a hero.) He was already envisioning a dramatic ceremony in which he personally would give the city back to the South Koreans. But first there was a battle to win. On September 19, General Smith discussed the crossing of the Han River which was to take place the next day. The Han River was a major barrier to the taking of Seoul. Smith noted that the requirements for crossing the Han River far exceeded the bridging material on hand. What was available was what the Marines themselves were bringing with them.

The crossing of the Han River was brushed off by General Edward Almond. He had a habit of treating the Han River like it had five or six intact bridges across it and, of course, it had none. Weeks later the X Corps still had no bridging materials to offer and the Marines would be forced to cross their men in amtracs, and their tanks on improvised ferries made from their own bridging material. The next day the 1st Marines attacked Yomdong-po, a populous suburb across the river from Seoul. The Quick approach to Seoul, and word that the North Koreans were crumbling around the Pusan perimeter infused the senior command with a sense of euphoria. On one trip to the front, MacArthur waiving his hand at the hills in the distance that surrounded Seoul, had assured that the enemy would simply dissolve before him. He left and returned to Tokyo that evening. General Almond assumed command of the X Corps. The battle for Seoul is a source of lasting controversy on many levels. A Great deal of it stems from the fact that MacArthur wanted the city liberated three months to the day after it was captured by the North Koreans, putting the final touch of the brilliance of Inchon. Almond had a slavish devotion to MacArthur and his greatest weakness as a commander in Korea was his conviction that MacArthur could do no wrong. Almond had little concern for conventional tactical doctrine that called for a division to be employed as a cohesive unit mutually supporting elements. He loved to create and send off small task forces on independent missions beyond other friendly units' support. He was forever pursuing the capture of real estate for its supposed psychological value, its publicity value, or to be the one commander in Korea who gave MacArthur precisely what he wanted first. The Marines were entering the city of Seoul and the enemy was putting up a bitter defense. Unfortunately Almond and his staff tended to see the problem not in terms of enemy resistance but of unduly slow process of the Marine division. Almond was trying to serve General MacArthur's preference for capturing Seoul as soon as possible, for maximum effect on the enemy and for the opportunity that this would give him to return the Government of the South Korean Republic and Syngman Rhee to the original capital city. The Marines were still fighting a bitter, desperate street battle for possession of the city that would go on for two more days. They faced intersections barred by chest high barricades made of rice and fiber bags filled with dirt and manned by enemy tanks and machine guns. The fighting was fierce and it took 3 days to clean out the city from the 25th to the 28th. So the North Koreans were not precipitously retreating from the city as Almond had reported. Shortly before midnight on the 25th, Almond reported that the city was liberated, MacArthur, following suit the next day in Tokyo, sent a communiqué which said in part: "Three months to the day after the North Koreans launched their surprised attack south of the 38th parallel our troops captured the city of Seoul. The enemy is fleeing the city to the north."

From the Marine point of view, the next three days bore no relationship to this version of the battle.

The final political note came at the ceremony in which MacArthur officially, and with great flourish, turned the city back to the South Koreans as represented by Syngman Rhee. The North Korean Army was on the run, hammered by both the 8th Army and the victorious Marines who had pushed the invaders out of Seoul. Only 25,000 North Koreans survived and were retreating north.

MacArthur's next move was for the 8th Army to push north to capture Pyongyang, the capital of North Korea. Once again, the command in Korea would be split with General Almond in control of the Marines on the east coast and General Walker in control of the 8th Army on the west. General Walker was not happy with this split command. He had been led to believe that the X-Corp would be united under his command once the capture of Seoul had been completed. Even General Almond had been told that when he was given the X-Corps, it would be just for the Inchon landing. General Walker protested to MacArthur that General Almond could not hold down both Chief of Staff and command the X-Corps. MacArthur said we will all be home for Christmas and, therefore, it is only a short operation and the 8th Army will become the controlling factor as soon as we capture the port of entry.

It became clear that General MacArthur was going to keep General Almond in command of both. He was a favorite of General MacArthur who would report and follow orders from MacArthur no matter what. This was the United States Army against MacArthur's Army. The immediate concern, however, was the matter of crossing the 38th parallel.

MacArthur asked the Joint Chief of Staff for permission to cross so that the North Koreans would be destroyed and rendered unable to invade the South again. The Joint Chief of Staff and President Truman agreed but with certain constrains. MacArthur was free to operate north of the 38th parallel provided that there had been no entry into North Korea by major Soviet or Chinese Communist forces, and only South Korean forces were to approach the Yalu river, which was the border between China and North Korea. Truman was caught up in the sweep of North Korea as was the Supreme Commander MacArthur who felt that this would be the crowning achievement to a brilliant career. Plans were under way for the landing at Pusan. When the landing happened, General Smith was instantly faced with what would be the wide dispersal of his division, typical of General Almond's approach. The units of his Division covered a zone of action that ran three hundred miles from north to south and sixty miles from east to west. Smith felt that it meant a loss of operational integrity but General Almond turned a deaf ear.

This dispersal of UN forces was occurring not only in the X Corps but in MacArthur's command as a whole. His forces were moving north toward the Yalu River along many different routes, which meant that they were not only incapable of mutual support but also of maintaining even limited ground patrol contact. This splitting of forces disturbed many at the Pentagon, General Omar Bradley in particular expressing concern over the vulnerability of the 8th Army's right flank and its distance from the X Corps.

The landing at Wonsan had brought a whiff of the winter weather that was soon to come. The first snows of winter had already fallen in the mountains to the north where the temperature was below freezing at night. These units heading north were the first to be outfitted with mountain sleeping bags, parkas, shoepacks, wind-proof trousers, ski socks and gloves.

In an era of high tech windproof and waterproof clothing, it is hard to imagine the equipment that was issued to those Marines headed for the arctic cold on the roof of the world. The parkas was a hooded heavy coat that came down to the knees, more suited for standing watch on a deck of a ship than marching or assaulting hills. While it was warm, its weight, when added to the weight of packs and weapons, was a great hindrance to movement. The shoepack, which was the winter boot, was made entirely of rubber. It cut off ventilation so that the foot would begin to perspire when the wearer was active, and when he ceased moving the accumulated sweat inside the boot would freeze causing frostbite.

The only feasible precaution for this was for men to change their socks frequently, while also attempting to dry the felt in the inner sole of the boot. Of course in the midst of combat this was seldom possible. One Marine noting that after a battle, "I took my shoepack off and found ice formed on the inside." Marines carried their sleeping bags rolled and tied to the bottom of their haversacks and were good for sleeping and keeping from freezing to death. The only problem was the temptation for Marines, who were allowed to pull their bags up to their knees while standing watch in foxholes to slip further in the bags and fall asleep. Sudden attack from the Chinese caused more than one Marine to be caught and killed in their sleeping bag.

On November 1, General Smith made a trip by helicopter to see the 7th Marines who was now in Hamhung. While there, an Republic of Korea (ROK) regiment had identified that they believed two Chinese regiments were in front of them. They were leaving the area and apparently had no stomach for fighting Chinese. General Smith and Commander Litzenberg were concerned about Chinese troops in the area but they were among the few. At the time, they did not know that they were already surrounded by a Chinese division.

The Chinese were keeping a close eye in the developments in Korea. Moa Tse Dong stated that the Chinese would not stand aside if the U.N. forces invaded the territory of their neighbor. He informed the Indian ambassador on October 5 that if the American troops crossed the 38th parallel, China would enter the war. This message was passed on to Washington and from there to Tokyo. MacArthur considered the statement merely a bluff, telling President Truman that there was very little chance that the Chinese would enter the war. We are no longer fearful of their intervention. We no longer stand hat in hand. As he was making this statement, 120,000 Chinese were already inside the border of North Korea.

Quoting from the book, **China's Road to the Korean War** by Chen Jian, some background on China, prior to the invasion of Korea became available. The Chinese leaders were convinced that the United States was too vulnerable to send any American troops to stop the Chinese from invading Taiwan.

The Chinese planned to invade Taiwan and liberate it and unify all of China and end its civil war and complete the destruction of the Nationalist Party (GMD). Their defeat in their attempt to occupy two small islands, Quemoy and Dengbu, that were offshore islands of Taiwan forced Chairman Mao to change their original plan for the Taiwan campaign.

On January 5, 1950, President Truman proclaimed that the United States would not challenge the notion that Taiwan was part of China. One week later, Secretary of State Acheson openly excluded Taiwan and South Korea from the United States western Pacific defense perimeter. The Chinese Leadership were then confident that Washington would not risk a third World War by sending troops to protect Taiwan.

In 1946, during the battle with the National forces in Manchuria, it was necessary to use North Korea as a strategic rear bases for the Communist forces in Southern Manchuria

The North Korean Communists assisted the Chinese not only with their setting up bases in North Korea, but in 1947 many North Korean soldiers joined the Chinese army to liberate China.

North Korea's backing dramatically strengthened the Chinese Communist strategic position in China's civil war. The Chinese leaders understood this and did not forget the "brotherly support" they had received from the North Korean Communists. In fact, the Chinese leaders used the North Korean support of the Chinese revolution to justify their decision to send troops to resist America and assist North Korea.

Chen Jian stated in his book that the response to the Korean War changed the scenario of the Chinese Mainland and also changed Taiwan's confrontation across the Taiwan Strait. President Truman sent the $7^{th}$ Fleet and maintained that the task was a neutral one. But the United States had virtually re-entered China's civil war on Taiwan's behalf, postponing their Taiwan campaign. The Chinese felt that the presence of the $7^{th}$ Fleet was a possible invasion of China proper and postponed the thought of invading Taiwan at this time.

Mao Tze Dong and the Chinese Communist Party issued the following statement: "President Truman of the United States, on June 27, intervened in the Korean Civil War and used Naval forces to control the Taiwan Strait in an attempt to stop our liberation of Taiwan.

The Chinese leadership determined that if the American Forces crossed the $38^{th}$ parallel into North Korea, they had no alternative but to enter into the war because American Forces at the Yalu River was a definite threat to the invasion of China proper.

Again quoting from the book **China's Road to the Korean War**, China's entry into the war immediately altered the balance of power on the Korean battlefield. The Chinese Army adopted a strategy of inducing the enemy troops to march forward and then eliminating them by superior forces striking them from the rear and on their flanks. On October 25, the Chinese Army initiated its first campaign in Korea, suddenly attacking South Korean troops in the Unsan area. In 12 days, South Korean troops were forced to retreat from areas close to the Yalu River to the Chongchun River. According to Chinese statistics, about 15,000 South Korean soldiers were killed in this campaign.

This setback should have sent a strong warning to the U.N. forces, but General MacArthur was too arrogant to heed it. He, like many policy makers in Washington, underestimated the size and determination of his Chinese adversaries. In mid-November, he decided to initiate a new "end the war" offensive. Considering MacArthur's aggressiveness and the fact that the Chinese heavy equipment remained on the North Bank of the Yellow River, the Chinese General Peng adopted a strategy of purposely showing ourselves to be weak, increasing the arrogance of the enemy, letting them run amuck and luring them deep into our areas. He ordered all Chinese units to retreat for about 30 kilometers to occupy favorable positions and to wait for the best opportunity to strike. In late November, advancing U.N. Forces entered areas where Chinese troops had laid their trap. Starting on November 25, Chinese Troops began a vigorous counter-offensive. Under tremendous pressure, U.N. troops had to undertake what the political scientist, Jonathan Pollack, has called "the most infamous retreat in American military history." By mid-December, the Chinese and the reorganized North Korean troops had regained control of nearly all North Korean territory.

In light of the achievements of the Chinese first two campaigns in Korea, Chairman Mao re-emphasized the original goal of "eliminating the enemy troops and forcing the Americans out of the Korean peninsula." He refused to consider any proposal about ending the Korean conflict through negotiations, and was determined to solve the Korean problem by winning a clear military victory. On December 21, he ordered General Peng "to fight another campaign and to cross the 38th parallel."

On the last day of 1950, the Chinese troops started the third campaign, and the U.N. Forces again retreated. Seoul fell to Chinese and North Korean troops on January 4, 1951. Concluding that Beijing's war effort was progressing smoothly, the North Korean leaders and Soviet advisers in Korea pushed General Peng to develop the offensive into one to end the war by total victory. With their supply lines extended and casualties increased, however the Chinese offensive gradually bogged down. Before the Chinese and North Koreans had an opportunity to coordinate their strategies, the U.N. Forces began a counter offensive in mid-January. On January 27, General Peng, with his troops exhausted and short of ammunition and food, proposed a tactical retreat to Chairman Mao. But the Chairman was not willing to consider anything short of a total victory. The next day, he ordered General Peng back on the offensive but the Chinese counter offensive was quickly repulsed by the U.N. Forces.

General Peng returned to Beijing to convey to Chairman Mao, in person, the real situation on the battlefield. Chairman Mao's ideas on Chinese strategy in Korea began to change. He now acknowledged that the war would be prolonged, and the best strategy was to rotate Chinese troops in and out of Korea.

After 2 months of readjustments and preparations, the Chinese and North Korean High Command gathered 12 armies to start an overall offensive in late April, planning to destroy the bulk of U.N. forces, and to establish clear Communist superiority on the battlefield. Without adequate air cover and reliable logistical supplies, this offensive failed. In the last stage of the campaign, several Chinese units that had penetrated too deeply into the U.N. front were surrounded by counter-attacking U.N. forces. One Chinese division and the 180th Division were totally lost.

The cruel reality forced Beijing leaders to reconsider China's war aims and they were willing to accept a "cease fire".

Returning to Marine General Olive Smith's report before the insertion of the book by Chen Jian it was determined that the intervention by the Chinese was ignored until it was too late. This information had many contributing factors. First of all, the Army Generals, and MacArthur, in particular had a low opinion of Chinese soldiers. The Chinese soldiers crossed eighteen mountain ranges and twenty four rivers averaging twenty four miles a day for 235 days. That such large numbers of Chinese troops could cross the border largely unnoticed by daily American reconnaissance flights was a result of their marching only between 9 pm and 3 am, during daylight every man, weapon, and pack animal were carefully hidden.

Aggravating the failure of American reconnaissance to confirm the Chinese presence was the fact that MacArthur and his G-2 did not want to believe that the Chinese were there. When confronted with evidence from Chinese prisoners, they would just dismiss them as Chinese volunteers. It should be remembered that MacArthur had a free rein in North Korea as long as there was no evidence of Chinese or Soviet intervention. MacArthur was pushing his troops toward the Yalu River and wanting nothing to come between him and his goal. Commenting "We will land and I will crush them. If the Chinese cross the Yalu River, I shall make of them the greatest slaughter in the history of mankind."

General Smith noted that the widely disbursed disposition by the X-Corps Marines was based on the assumption that we were pursuing a defeated North Korean Army. The intervention of the Chinese Army was discounted. There was an estimated 27 divisions of between 250,000 and 300,000 men massed just north of the Yalu River. MacArthur said that they were not coming across the border and General Almond, as always, was a true believer of MacArhur.

Then suddenly on November 1, reality struck when the Chinese attacked an ROK Division on the right flank of the 8th Army, engulfing them so completely that they ceased to exist. With the right flank gone, the Chinese then fell on the 8th Calvary at Unsan. Taken completely by surprised in spite of the many warnings that Chinese troops were in the area, the regiment lost more than 600 men, half of them taken prisoner, including a number of wounded that were left behind. They also lost 9 tanks, 12 howitzers and 150 assorted vehicles that fell into enemy hands.

One day later, in the X-Corps zone of action it was the 7th Marines who faced the Chinese in force, but with very different results. Marching north from Hamhung, the Marines met heavy resistance outside the town of Sudong. The Chinese were repulsed suffering heavy losses.

The 7th Marines had faced the 124th Chinese division and in 5 days of heavy fighting had rendered it non-combat effective. In the process, the Marines had lost 44 killed 5 dead of wounds, one missing and 162 wounded. The Chinese suffered over 1,000 dead with a number of unknown wounded, It would be several months before that Division would appear at the front again.

After a moment of shock, MacArthur regained his optimism believing that the disaster at Unsan was simply caused by a lack of pickets. The UN troops were again urged forward toward the Yalu River.

These two confrontations represented the last chance for MacArthur to reconsider his plans before the Chinese Army would attack in force. In the intervening years as Chinese records have been open to western scholars, it had been discovered that those attacks on the 8th Army and the X-Corps were meant as a signal to the Americans that the Chinese intended to fight if the advance toward the Yalu River was continued. In the unrealistic atmosphere of his court in Tokyo, one field commander having no access to the throne and the other devoted beyond the ability to act independently, MacArthur ignored the warning and pushed toward the Yalu River.

For one person, however, this action against the 7th Marines was a warning that was taken seriously. On November 7, General Smith met with General Almond and felt that the attack by the Chinese had been a blocking action meant to delay his division in its march north while the enemy brought more forces to bear. General Smith's division was dispersed over 170 miles from Wonsan in the south to Chinghung in the north, and should be consolidated because this division is fighting a sizeble unit of Chinese Communist Army.

General Smith was intensely proud of his Marine division's fighting ability, and more than ready to wield it in battle. He was not about to see his Marines thrown away in a wild rush to the Chinese border that ignored the danger signals that were so obvious to him. There would be no thoughtless waste of troops ordered by a Commanding General whose grasp on reality had slipped. This would not be another Peleliu. Over the course of the next month, this determination would save his division. But his action would come with a high professional cost for General Smith.

General Smith now focused on three priorities. The first was the main supply route in which the bulk of traffic in support of his Division flowed. His second focus was on his exposed left flank. When the 8th Army had suffered reverses at the hands of the Chinese in the first day of November, it had been forced to fall back, and although it had regained its equilibrium it was still not advancing. The distance between the First Marine Division and the 8th Army was 60 air miles. Yet, General Almond in his continuing desire to please MacArthur, kept up the pressure for the 7th Marines to make rapid progress toward the reservoir, which would only serve to widen the distance between the two forces.

Smith's third focus was on concentrating his forces. In a meeting with General Almond on November 7th, General Smith urged that the situation be reviewed; that in view of the approach of winter, consideration should be given to stop the advance to the North. He recommended that during the winter months the X Corps commit itself only to holding enough terrain to provide for the security of the coastal force and not attempt to hold positions on the high mountain plateaus. General Almond had promised to let General Smith concentrate on the First Marine Division but, on November 11, the X-Corps was directed to advance to the Yalu River.

On the night of November 10, the bottom fell out of the thermometer, and the Marines experienced temperatures which dropped from 32 degrees Fahrenheit to minus 8 degrees, accompanied by 20 to 30 knot winds. The weather would become a large factor for the Marines. The water froze in their canteens and rations froze in their packs. Because of lack of calories, some men would report as much as 15 to 20 pounds weight loss during the course of the campaign. Plasma froze so that it and other medical supplies had to be kept near roaring stoves to be effective. As for equipment, guns froze solid and had to have all the oil removed to make them functional again. Automatic weapons would often fire only one or two rounds before jamming. Helicopters were initially put out of service as the controls froze.

The Army's $3^{rd}$ Division was finally directed to relieve the $1^{st}$ Marines at Wonsan. General Smith now hoped to close them up behind the $5^{th}$ and $7^{th}$ Marines, but General Almond, his confidence returning in direct proportion to the returning confidence of MacArthur in Tokyo, had other plans for them. The Marines were to take off on an offensive operation on another tangent to the West, entirely separate from the drive North the rest of the Division was making toward the reservoir. On November 14, General Smith had a conference with General Almond where he pointed out to him the anomaly of the situation when we were making a main effort to the North via the Chosen Reservoir. And, at the same time, were required to prepare to attack many miles south of the Chosen Reservoir. General Almond relented, but he was still urging the other two regiments to push forward quickly. General Almond was saying, "We've got to go barreling up that road."

General Smith's involuntary response was: "NO!" General Almond pretended not to hear it. After he departed, General Smith said: "We're not going anywhere until I get this Division together and an airfield built."

Thus began General Smith's conscious decision to slow down the advance of his Marines going northward. This was the one thing that he could do for his division. He was slowing his advance not only to close up his division but to create stockpiles of needed supplies along the way. Fortified base camps were gradually established as the column wound its way up into the mountains. Each of these camps were nestled behind well sited perimeter defenses and had supporting artillery able to fire in any direction and build an airstrip. All of these preparations by General Smith's foresight were ultimately the results of saving thousands of Marines and the Marine division as a whole.

General Almond was not happy with General Smith and expressed his dissatisfaction with the division's progress. But General Smith continued to slow down the advance.

On November 21, General Smith received news that the 3rd Infantry Division was to relieve the 1st Marines. This allowed General Smith to move the 1st Marines up the mountain to relieve units of the 5th and 7th so that the 2 units were able to consolidate all their units.

General Almond directed that the 5th and 7th Marines go up the side of the Chosin Reservoir. The whole situation looked bad to General Smith and his commanders. General Smith hoped that there would be a change of orders on the conservative side but it did not come. One more additional fact that came to General Smith's growing list of danger signals was that the bridge at Funchilin pass was still intact. The Chinese, in their retreat north after the battle with the 7th Marines, earlier in the month, had not blown the bridge. With the impassable cliff one side and a chasm on the other, a blown bridge would have delayed the march of our troops toward the Yalu River. General Smith was sure that they wanted us to come across and then blow the bridge thus completely isolating us.

On November 24, MacArthur flew from Tokyo to the 8th Army headquarters for the offensive that would end the war. The 8th Army and the X Corps were to form 2 giant pincers, separated by the unpatrolled high mountainous spine of the peninsular of as much as 50 air miles in some spots. The 8th Army was to move northward in the west and center while the X Corps was to strike northwest to cut off the enemy supply line and eventually link up with the 8th Army at the Yalu River.

On the 24th of November, the first intimation of the disaster to come from the 8th Army after being sent off by General MacArthur, the 8th Army advanced 3 Corps abreast along a 50 mile front preceded by the heaviest artillery barrage of the war. In zero degree temperature, roads glazed over with ice and savage north winds made quick gains the first day bearing out MacArthur's confidence. The next morning, the Chinese counter attacked and the various units began to fall apart.

The Army would begin the longest retreat of American warfare. In light of what was happening in the west, General Smith found that the mission of the 1st Marine Division had been changed. Now that disaster had struck, General MacArthur ordered General Almond to reorient his attack. Instead of heading to the Yalu River, the Marines were to attack west to assist the 8th Army which was almost a hundred miles away.

The division found this new order unrealistic. Col. Alpha Bowser the G3 called it "goofy," Commander Raymond Murray called it "crazy," and even General Ruffer, the X Corps Chief of Staff, called the plan "insane." General Smith would say that the mission to fight 40 miles to the west through 80,000 Chinese troops was absolutely impossible. The Joint Chief of Staff (JCS) made only one final, feeble attempt to stay General MacArthur's hand. Instead, General

MacArthur had flown to the 8$^{th}$ Army headquarters to launch the decisive attack. General Smith left Yudam-ni and his two regiments knowing that the situation was "ominous". The interrogation of prisoners indicated that the enemy was present in force.

What General Smith did not know and was not told was the extent of the disaster unfolding to the west. The right flank of the 8$^{th}$ Army and the ROK 11 Corps had been crushed by the Chinese Army the day before, causing the rest of the 8$^{th}$ Army to withdraw and that withdrawal was fast becoming a retreat. As General Smith flew back to his division headquarters at Hamhung, he looked at the stretch of road over which his Marines were strung out. Invisible from the air or the ground was the Chinese Army moving in to fall on the Marine division. In fact, 8 divisions of Chinese against General Smith's one division was dangerous.

In late November, the Chinese army's Political Commissars would tell their troops near the Chosin Reservoir, "Soon we will meet American Marines in battle and we will destroy them. When they are defeated, they will collapse and our country will be free from the treat of aggression. Kill these Marines as you would kill snakes in your home. Radio Peking would trumpet "The annihilation of the United States Marine Division is only a matter of time."

In spite of what Tokyo knew to be the rapidly disintegrating situation in the west, on the morning of November 27, the 2$^{nd}$ Battalion, 5th Marines, attacked to the west as schedule. The 7$^{th}$ Marines were charged with holding the hills around Yudam-ni.

Fighting the first day was fierce and the Marine advances were modest. Night came and the temperature dropped to minus 20 degrees. Trigger fingers, even though heavily gloved, ached against the metal, parka hoods were covered with frost, and feet in shoepacs became aching lumps of ice. While Marines sat frozen and immobile in their foxholes, the hills were alive with advancing Chinese. The battles that took place from this point can be read in the books **For Country and Corps** and the book **CHOSIN** by Eric Hammel. Also the book **THE RIVER AND THE GAUNTLET**, the defeat of the 8$^{th}$ Army by the Chinese Communist Forces in November of 1950 relates to this subject.

# BREAKOUT

On the 29th of November, the Army Tank Company east of the reservoir made one more attempt to reach the two infantry and artillery battalions to the north. Once again, they were unable to pass Hill 1221, which was heavily defended by the Chinese.

In the evening of November 29, General Smith heard from X Corps Headquarters that General Almond had been called to Tokyo for a secret meeting with MacArthur. General Almond then returned to his Command Post and issued new orders that all Army elements in the area were immediately put under General Smith's command. When all broke loose, and it was obvious that the Division had been placed in an extremely dangerous position. The Corps was then turned over to me and I was given command of everything in the general area of the Chosin Reservoir and south.

In addition to bringing out the Marine Division, I was held responsible for the extrication and safety of the two battalions of Infantry and Artillery of the 7th Division and to extricate the Army units of the east of the Chosin Reservoir plus concentrate on his Division at Hagaru-ri.

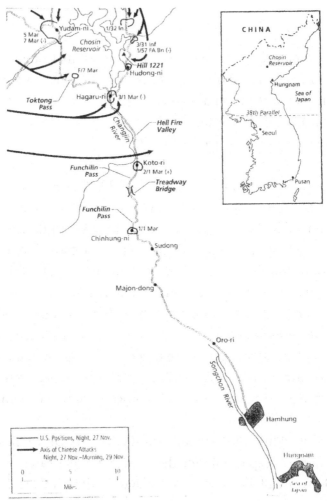

The Chosin Reservoir, December 1950

General Almond could have corrected his poor judgment if he had listened to his Commanders both in the Army and Marines, and taken true measure of the situation. One can only imagine the lives that would have been saved if General Almond had given the orders for not only the Army regiment east of the Chosin Reservoir but to the Marine Regiment to fall back two days earlier. Now that everyone was in trouble, particularly the Army troops, General Almond simply turned the whole mess over to General Smith with a phone call.

General Almond visited headquarters and told the press that the action now in progress is an entirely new Chinese development and that the defeat of the North Koreans had virtually been accomplished. Once again reflecting, General MacArthur's spin on the deluge now being faced by the UN troops when he stated "We are fighting an entirely new war." General Almond says, with a wave of the hand, that we are to go back south with all speed and to destroy all supplies and equipment.

The complete unreality of General Almond's statement, made in a Command Post (CP) a few hundred yards from where Thomas Ridge's Marines were still contending for the position of East Hill, must have stunned his listeners. General Smith told General Almond that "My movement would be governed by my ability to evacuate the wounded and I would have to fight my way back and could not afford to discard any equipment, and that I intend to bring out the bulk of my equipment." From December 1 through December 5, 4,312 wounded men would be flown out. General Smith directed the withdrawal south to Hagaru-ri. It was at this point that the press discovered what was going on in the mountains of North Korea and almost missed the compelling story that was unfolding there. Reporting on the situation that now faced the Marines, General Smith felt that they had missed the real crisis.

All along it seem strange to me that there has been a tendency to treat the movement south down the mountains as if these things were the crisis of the operation. This simply was not the case. The advance of the two returning regiments was the real crisis. The afternoon of December 4 brought the last of the 5th Marines into Hagaru-ri. The arrival of the press at the airfield brought two interesting sidelights. It was a British correspondent who was the genesis for the famous quote attributed to General Smith. "Retreat hell, we are just advancing in a different direction." He came to General Smith to ask whether he should title the operation a "retreat or a withdrawal." General Smith told him it was neither, since the division was completely surrounded and would have to fight its way out. The press immediately improved on this statement and "Retreat hell" was born.

General Smith now prepared for the next phase. There was no word of any withdrawal. This was an attack order and, on December 6 all of the 10,020 men would break out of Hagaru-ri toward Koto-ri. They had to fight their way through nine roadblocks by the Chinese. The Chinese had blown bridges along the way and on one occasion it was impossible to repair the bridge. Lt. Col John Partridge, Commander of the Engineer Battalion, flew over the site and his plan was to have the Air Force drop sections of treadway spans at Koto-ri, which the engineers would install once the bridge had been captured from the Chinese.

The Air Force responded to what they called a remarkable request. The eight spans were loaded into a C-119 and two huge G-5 parachutes were hitched to the end of each span. The bridge spans were dropped in the morning of December 7. At the same time, two Brockway trucks came up the Main Supply Route (MSR) that had winches made for handling the bridge sections. With the trucks came a young Army Lieutenant with experience in the construction of treadway bridges. Now that the bridging materials were in place, the problem was that the bridge site was in enemy hands. The next step was the most complex and it involved that the 5th and 7th Marines would fight down toward Funchilin Pass taking not only the road but also the high ground on either side of the road.

The 1st Battalion would fight up the mountain from the south with the object of taking Hill 1081 which dominated the pass and the bridge. When the road and high ground were cleared of enemy, then the Brockway trucks would be brought up and the bridge spans put in place. After some problems in completing the bridge and holding off the enemy, the convoy started across.

The first Marine Division had fought the best the Chinese could throw at them as well as the worst of the North Korean weather. They had battled their way down the mountains in two weeks of grim, intense and inspired fighting. In some ways, the skill and bravery they showed defied rational explanation, the fortitude awing even the hardest veterans.

The Marines poured into the port of Hungham battle scared and filled with tremendous pride. For thirteen days they had been at the world's center stage as they fought their way out of the winter fastness of the North Korean mountains and into history. The Marine Division fighting night and day and aided during the daylight hours by Marine and Naval close air support cut its way through 7 Chinese divisions and parts of 3 others which attempted to destroy it. The Marines came through their 13 day ordeal with units intact, with their weapons and equipment and all of their wounded.

Congratulations began to pour in from around the world from the Admiralty in London and many of General Smith's superiors including even General MacArthur in a report to the United Nations called the march "epic." Even the president got in on the act, quoted in the New York Times "This last withdrawal from the Chosin Reservoir was one of the greatest fighting retreats that ever was. Perhaps the best description of the operation and its Commander comes from an article written five years later by S.L.A. Marshall upon General Smith's retirement. The Chosin Reservoir campaign is perhaps the most brilliant Division feat of arms in the national history. Smith made it so, through his dauntless calm, his tender regard for his Marines and his unshakable belief that rest when needed rather than to precipitate haste, was the only thing which would bring his men through the greatest of combat trials.

The aftermath of the Chosin Reservoir campaign would change. It marked the end of the 1st Marine Division's service under General Almond. Major General Frank Lowe wrote to President Truman that it would be much for the interest of the service to never again require the 1st Marine Division to serve under General Almond's command. And General Ridgeway himself would later promise General Smith that the 1st Marine Division would not again be put under General Almond.

General Almond retained his command, as General MacArthur could not afford to criticize someone who had exactly followed his every instruction. General Almond never admitted any culpability for his rush to the Yalu River, either for the position that he had placed the 1$^{st}$ Marine Division or, more importantly, the destruction of the 8$^{th}$ Army. He found fault with both Ridgeway and Collin's books as well as with the official Army history of the Korean War.

A facet of the post Chosin River world would be the matter of the Presidential unit citation that was awarded to the 1$^{st}$ Marine Division for the Chosin Reservoir operation. It would be one of three that the Marine division would earn in Korea, the other two being for the Inchon-Seoul campaign and for operations in central Korea in 1951. The Navy awarded the unit citation for Inchon and General Ridgeway made sure that the division received it for its work in Central Korea. It became apparent that the X Corps had no interest in giving out a unit award for the Chosin Reservoir operation. Month after month followed with no interest from the Army in considering the award. General Smith wrote to Brigadier General Lemuel Shepherd about the problem of official recognition of the Division as a unit for an Army citation. General Shepherd knew, as well as General Smith, that politics were involved in the issue. And General Almond was pursuing anything that would add to General Smith's luster even at the expense of an entire division. In 1953, the Navy would recommend the award. As there were certain Army units included in the award, General Smith said that the Army made an effort to ring in several units, which played no significant part in the breakout of the 1st. Marine Division. Interestingly, in the light of future developments, the unit that the Army was pushing for inclusion were those of the Army after withdrawal from the Chosin Reservoir to give credit to the 3rd Infantry Division for rescuing the 1st Marine Division. They portrayed the Marines as having gotten themselves in a situation beyond their control. These Army units had been brought forward solely to relieve the Marines so that the Marines could take the hills that dominated Funchilin Pass.

S.L.A. Marshall wrote that all of Army Lt. Colonel Smuck's Battalion were exceedingly indignant about stories which, credited the 3rd Infantry Division for having rescued the 1st Marine Division and giving General Soule, Commander of the 3rd Infantry Division the Distinguish Service Cross for having commanded the 3rd Infantry Division during this effort. Lt. Colonel Smuck pointed out that it was the fighting done by his Battalion which lifted the last heavy pressure from the Marine Division's back and that had been done according to plan. It seems to me that this view of the case is adequately sustained by the record that the words "according to plan," fit the 1st Marine Division operation throughout, despite a smoke screen attempt by the Army to make it appear that the Marines were extricated from a situation that had gotten beyond their control. General Smith commented that the Army had fought its way 45 miles to our rescue. This is simply dishonest publicity on the part of the 3rd Division. I would think that they would squirm when they read it.

One survivor of the 3rd Battalion unit summed it up: It was always my opinion that the Army High Command was not proud of the operation on the east side of the Chosin Reservoir. Since that operation provided textbook examples of every conceivable type of command and staff failure humanly possible, their reaction was to sweep it under the rug and forget it. In fact, an official Army history of that period of the Korean War was not even published until 1990. However, General Smith did not ignore men of the Marine Regiment Combat Team 31 and gave credit to those who were not evacuated from Hagaru-ri but formed a battalion that fought its way down the mountain with the Marines. They were included in the award along with that of the tank company that had participated in the defense of Hagaru-ri. The matter lied dormant for years, but in 1990 a movement was begun to include all of the RCT 31 in the presidential unit citation which was finally accomplished in 2000. For the survivors and various historians to completely ignore the three Army Generals Almond, Barr, and Hodges, not to mention MacArthur, who among them placed an Army unit in harm's way without sufficient logical support, proper equipment, and functioning communication is bewildering.

Returning to the withdrawal to the port of Hamhung on December 14, all the ships carrying the 1st Marine Division were loaded and the convoy sailed the next day with 99,000 military personnel, 17,780 vehicles, 11,000 tons of cargo and 100,000 refugees were evacuated. General Smith had always been interested in defeating the enemy in the field and had wrecked havoc on the Chinese divisions that faced him. In figures that were later confirmed, the Chinese suffered 37,500 battle casualties—22,500 by Marine ground forces and 15,000 by air and one third of the remaining forces were disabled by the cold weather. The commander of the Chinese 9th Army commented only "They are gone, we could not stop them." For the same period, the Marines suffered 4,418 battle casualties of whom 604 were killed in action, 144 died of wounds and 192 were missing in action. Of the 3,150 that were evacuated, about 1,200 suffered serious Frost bites and the rest were wounded.

Quoting Lt Col. Kenneth W. Estes, USMC (RET) Editor of Marine officer's guide 7th edition. Stating about the important information about an iconic Marine Corps leader who worked and studied hard and demonstrated a masterful leadership and tactical competence.

I believe that General Smith's knowledge of warfare and that he took actions not only to protect his Marines but to save the 1st Marine Division from the same fate that destroyed the 8th Army. The Army Generals would berate the Marine Corps and continue to further attempt to destroy them. I strongly recommend that anyone who is interested in knowing what happened in Korea and the trap that General MacArthur and General Almond was sending the 1st Division of the Marine Corps into just to enhance MacArthur's ego trip, should read the book <u>FOR COUNTRY AND CORPS</u>.

In the book, <u>AMERICAN CAESAR,</u> the story of Douglas MacArthur by William Manchester evaluates MacArthur's life and writes about the many good things he has done, but also about his many failures. Manchester states that he was a great thundering paradox of a man, noble and ignoble, inspiring and outrageous, arrogant and shy, the best of men and the worst of men, the most protean, most ridiculous, and most sublime.

No more baffling, exasperating soldier that ever wore a uniform. Flamboyant, imperious, and apocalyptic, he carried the plumage of a flamingo, could not acknowledge errors, and tried to cover up his mistakes with sly childish tricks. Manchester presents MacArthur in all his many faceted glory, complexity, and contradictions. Here is MacArthur the military genius capable of masterpieces such as the landing at Inchon and inexplicable lapses (knowing that Pearl Harbor had been attacked, he let his Philippine air force be destroyed on the ground nine hours later by the Japanese.) He also wrote extensively about the many problems MacArthur caused in ordering troops into the mountains of North Korea in a winter blizzard. He also wrote about the execution of Japanese Generals Homma and Yamashita whom were both innocent.

I would like to further comment on General MacArthur's belief of his self-importance as I quote from the book A TRIAL OF GENERALS by Lawrence Taylor. When the American forces on Bataan surrendered to the Japanese in early 1942, both sides were astonished to discover that the Japanese under General Masaharu Homma had defeated General MacArthur's army more than twice its size. For the Japanese the 100,000 soldiers and civilians coming out of the jungles of the Philippines Bataan peninsula presented a horrendous logistical problem of how to get them into POW camps. The result was the infamous Bataan death march, during which 7,000 American servicemen succumbed to heat, disease, exhaustion and the brutalities of their captors.

During the Death March, General Homma was busy trying to capture the remaining American soldiers, first under General MacArthur and later after General

MacArthur's departure for Australia, and under General Jonathan Wainwright from their entrenched position on the island of Corregidor in Manila Bay. General Homma was to remain unaware of the atrocities being perpetrated by his troops until the end of the war.

By the end of 1944, the war was going badly for the Japanese, General MacArthur was mustering an overwhelming force to retake the Philippines. General Tomoyuki Yamashita, the hero of Japan's military Campaign, was hurriedly recalled from his post to shore up the weakened and frail defense of the island.

General Tomoyuki Yamashita's order was to pull back into the Philippine jungles, abandoning Manila as hopeless to sustain under an American onslaught. General Tomoyuki Yamashita issued orders to leave Manila and not to destroy it as he headed into the jungle.

But sailors under the command of Admiral Iwabuchi, apparently with his blessing and directly in the face of General Yamashita's orders, did not leave Manila. Instead they fortified themselves with alcohol and counting themselves as already dead, went on a rampage against Manila and its inhabitants raping, burning, torturing and murdering. General Tomoyuki Yamashita virtually isolated in the jungles, waited until the war's end to surrender. It was then that he heard about the incredible acts of sailors normally under his command. With the Allied victory came the Nuremberg and Tokyo war crimes tribunals. Both were models of due process, with internationally recognized jurists deliberating for years about the charges and counter charges involved. But long before this, these two Japanese Generals were tried in the Philippines by a military commission under General MacArthur.

They were found guilty, appealed that decision, lost, were executed. The book A TRIAL OF GENERALS is the first full treatment of these trials which were travesties of American judicial conduct. It tells the story not only of the background trials and executions. It also tells the human story of three generals caught in a desperate bind involving the highest calling of the military profession—duty, honor, country.

On September 2, 1945 General MacArthur accepted the Japanese surrender aboard the battleship Missouri in Tokyo Bay. It is my belief that Admiral Nimitz did more to defeat the Japanese by destroying its army, navy and air force and should have been the one to accept the Japanese surrender.

After the ceremonies were completed, he informed the general press: "As Supreme Commander for the allied powers, I announce it my firm purpose in the tradition of the countries I represent, to proceed in the discharge of my responsibilities with justice and tolerance." Standing ominously at his side as these words were being read were the two Allied Commanders who, along with General MacArthur, had suffered the most humiliating defeats of the war—General Wainright and the British General Percival.

MacArthur wasted no time in meeting out justice, if not tolerance. At the directive of the U.S. Joint Chiefs of Staff, MacArthur ordered the investigation and detention of all Japanese suspected of war crimes. It specifically empowered MacArthur to set up special international courts for the trial of those charged and to prescribe the rules of procedure to be followed by them. Armed with this authority, MacArthur quickly established two separate war crime offices.

The first was called the "International Prosecution Section" and was intended to bring to justice the major Japanese war criminals, starting with Hideki Tojo. To facilitate this prosecution, MacArthur created the International Military Tribunal for the Far East to sit in judgment in Tokyo.

Essentially, it was similar to the Nazi trials in Nuremburg and consisted of a panel of independent judges from eleven Allied Nations.

The second office set up by MacArthur was the War Crime Branch of the U.S. General Headquarters of the

Armed Forces in the Pacific, with branches based in Yokohama and Manila. The purpose of this military prosecution agency was to investigate and bring to trial all war criminals not considered "major" enough for the inclusion in the Tokyo trials. The judicial body for these trials was to consist of U.S. Army officers appointed by MacArthur. The difference between the procedure followed by the two separate war crimes system were considerable. Tojo and twenty seven other political and military leaders were afforded every conceivable procedural safeguards. The panel of judges was composed of brilliant legal minds, many of them from the supreme courts of their respected nations. Evidently, rules and legal procedure were strictly observed and no pressure was, or could be, brought to bear on the Justices. Aside from establishing the proceedings, MacArthur took little part.

The trials that were to take place in MacArthur's adopted home of Manila, however, were to prove another matter altogether. There the stage was quickly set for the trials of the two men responsible for Bataan and Manila.

General Tomoyuki Yamashita was charged with war crimes three weeks after the surrender and the trial was set to begin three weeks after that. Despite the awesome task for administrating the government of Japan, his attention was immediately directed to the prosecution of the two Japanese Generals. MacArthur turned first to the matter of General Yomoyuki Yamashita, for Manila was fresh in his mind. He quickly appointed six military lawyers from the Judge Advocate's Department to serve as the prosecution team. In fact this was done before the Japanese surrender. The sixth member was a political appointment. Mac Arthur felt that it was wise to give the Philipino people some representation in the prosecution. Opinion was, however, to prove a bumbling fool in the trial. MacArthur realized that a staff of defense lawyers would have to be appointed to represent General Yamashita but delayed it until the last moment. In fact the defense lawyers were not named until shortly before the arraignment. It was obvious that these newly appointed lawyers would not begin to put together a defense to sixty-two counts of war crimes, any one of which could be punishable by death. As one of the defense Attorneys later wrote "We knew that to make even a pretense of investigation of these crimes, involving thousands of people and hundreds of miles of territory, would take many months."

While the appointment of the defense team was held off, MacArthur directed the prosecution staff to begin drafting charges and gathering the evidence. They were given top priority of all supplies, manpower and transportation that was needed. And so, months before the Japanese had surrendered, teams of lawyers and investigators were combing the Philippines, gathering evidence to be used in the trial. This book, The Trial of Generals continues to explain the different persons on each side and it amazing how the quality of each individual was assigned, and the roadblocks that were thrown at the defense when they tried to make a case for the defense. Three more men were needed and they were finally appointed. One of them was Captain Frank Reel. When Captain Reel heard about the unwanted assignment, he called a friend in MacArthur's Judge Advocate section, Bill Ruddick, who had already seen the charges that had been prepared against Yamashita and had discussed some of the evidence with the prosecutors. "They have nothing on him at all." They're trying to establish a new theory—that a Commanding Officer is responsible if his troops violate the laws of war, regardless of whether he ordered the violations or even knew about them" He paused and then added;" under such a theory, I guess even General MacArthur should be tried."

MacArthur now turned to the composition of the tribunal itself. He would personally select five men to sit on the Military Commission in Manila. Predictably, MacArthur picked five members of the regular Army. Three Major Generals and two Brigadier Generals who would decide the outcome of the case. Five professional officers whose future career might well depend on offering no resistance to MacArthur's well known desires. This book goes on to describe the background of each of these, such as none of these were combat

Officers etc. MacArthur had personally selected the five judges, appointed the prosecutors and had delegated the selection of the defense lawyers. But MacArthur was not finished. He personally drafted the criminal procedure to be followed in conducting the trial as well as the rules of evidence that would be adhered to. General procedures established by Military Courts. Martial would not do, nor would civilian criminal procedures. The usual rules of evidence were considered "obstructionist," and the safeguard of the Constitution were ignored. Finally, MacArthur established a system of appeals from judgments of conviction, which were very simple. If a defendant was convicted and sentenced to death, there was only one source of appeal: General Douglas MacArthur. The trial was a farce, one of the correspondents covering the trial wrote Yamashita trial continues today, but it isn't a trial, I doubt that it is even a hearing. I urge you to read about this so-called trial in this book. When it was over, General Reynolds read from the papers before him.

General Yamashita: The commission concludes (1) a series of atrocities and other high crimes have been committed by members of the Japanese Armed Forces under your command against the people of the United States, their Allies, and dependencies throughout the Philippine Islands; that they were not sporadic in nature but in many cases were methodically supervised by Japanese officers and noncommissioned officers. (2)

During the period in question, you failed to provide effective control of your troops as was required by the circumstances. Accordingly, upon secret written ballots, two thirds or more of the members concurring, the commission finds you guilty as charged and sentences you to death by hanging.

The next "trial" moved on to the next Japanese General Masaharu Homma that began on January 3, 1946. It was to continue for one month, and, in many ways, indistinguishable in character or format from the trial of General Yamashita. The presence of any credible evidence pointing to General Homma's ordering any of the Atrocities, or to even knowing of their existence, was totally absent. Again, the prosecution was proceeding on a vague theory of negligence. The Prosecution could not prove that General Homma knew of any of the atrocities. Once again, the prosecution would ask for his execution because he should have known. There were further charges of violation of Manila's open city and the refusal to accept Wainwright's surrender. These were ridiculous charges to begin with. As the U.S. Army chief of Military History has since admitted that Manila was in fact not an open city: MacArthur still had kept troops in it and both he and Homma knew it. Similarly, Wainwright later admitted that he lied to General Homma about his authority at the initial surrender negotiations. Homma knew of the deceit and was absolutely correct in refusing to accept a surrender of anything less than Wainwright's complete command. It was, therefore, the Death March and the prison camps that became the focus of attention. General Homma was recalled to Japan before the camp situation happened. He was also preoccupied with the campaign against the almost impregnable fortress on Corregidor, leaving the subordinates in command, ordering them to treat all prisoners properly, giving them food and medical care. Again, the interrogation of General Homma can be read in this book. On February 11, 1946, at 3:00 p.m. the Commission returned a guilty verdict in the case of U.S.A. verses Masaharu Homma. The punishment was set of death by hanging. Serious charges have been raised about MacAthur's handling of the Commission but nothing came of it.

It is my own observation that General MacArthur proceeded with this procedure because of a vendetta. It was General Homma who had defeated General MacArthur's forces in the Philippines and it was General Yamashita who was the general when Manila was sacked and in the process destroying General MaCArthur's 6 room air-conditioned pent house with his trophies and library.

The book A TRIAL OF GENERALS, was written by Lawrence Taylor who is a criminal attorney in Los Angeles and has written other books and articles on trial matters.

# RESPECT

General Pershing should have apologized for his objections to the French High Command naming Belleau Wood as Bois de la Brigade de Marine.

The Army-dominated American Battle Monument Commission should apologize for refusing to honor over three hundred fallen Marine heroes buried in an out of the way cemetery and for refusing to allow a Marine Corps emblem or a statue of a Marine, or even a marker, to acknowledge this place as the Bois de la Brigade de Marine.

General MacArthur should have apologized for refusing to honor the Marines who fought at the Philippines by only putting in a Presidential citation award for the Army troops and refusing the award for the Marines because he stated, "they had their glory in World War I." He should have also apologized for the unnecessary casualties of 1,252 Marines killed and 2,736 wounded at Peleliu. because he was afraid of his Right flank when he returned to the Philippines which had no bearing his landing.

The Army should apologize for putting an Army General like General Edward Almond in charge of the

Marines in Korea, causing many unnecessary Marine casualties because of his ineptitude. An Army General should never be put in charge of Marines again.

The Army Generals should stop complaining about the Marines being used in Iraq and Afghanistan and should say "thank you" to the Marines for fighting alongside of the Soldiers.

The Navy should apologize to the Marines for abandoning them on the beaches at Guadalcanal, leaving them with only half of the supplies needed to fight the Japanese.

The Navy Bureau of Ships should apologize for opposing and delaying the produtction of the Higgins landing crafts that was the necessary part of amphibious landing by the Marines in the Pacific.

Congress should apologize for allowing the Eisenhower Administration of wrestling away its responsibility of having created the Marine Corps and being responsible for its existence when they allowed the creation of the position of Secretary of Defense which has control of the fate of the Marine Corps.

The Marine Corps should not have to fight for the right to fight to defend their country. They have proven to be a necessary part of the Armed Forces and should be recognized for their performance since their creation in 1775.

There is a saying, "Once a Marine, always a Marine." Once you have had the experience of being a Marine, it continues to run through your blood no matter how long you have been out of active service. All Marines, whether active or not, are proud to be part of what we call the finest fighting organization of the Military. We should stand together against all forces that attempt to minimize or degrade the service and the tradition of the Marine Corps.

'Well Done!'     By Sgt. George Ward

# INDEX